MANTRAS FOR THE EVENING

MANTRAS FOR THE EVENING

The Experience of Holistic Prayer

Robert F. Morneau

The Liturgical Press   Collegeville, Minnesota

Cover design by Placid Stuckenschneider, O.S.B.

ISBN: 0-8146-1269-5
Library of Congress Catalog Card Number: 82-83587.

CONTENTS

6 *Contents*

ACKNOWLEDGMENTS

The author acknowledges the generous and expert assistance of these people who contributed their time and talent to make this book possible: REV. ROBERT LALIBERTE (pp. 13, 21, 45, 49, 65, 90, 105); REV. JOHN BLAHA (pp. 33, 41, 69, 77, 85); MRS. NICKI DAVIS (pp. 17, 25, 29, 37, 53, 57, 61, 73, 81, 93, 97, 101, 109), for their photography; SISTER MIRIAM CECILE ROSS, S.S.N.D., for the music; SISTER MARY DE SALES HOFFMANN, O.S.F., and SISTER MARIE ISABEL MC-ELRONE, O.S.F., for editorial assistance; ROSEMARY ROBERTS, for typing.

Scripture texts used in this book are from *The Jerusalem Bible*, copyright © 1966 by Darton, Longman & Todd, Inc., and used by permission of the publisher.

Grateful acknowledgment is made to the following for permission to include excerpts of copyrighted material: DOUBLEDAY & COMPANY, INC.: *Reaching Out* by Henri J. M. Nouwen, copyright © 1975 by Henri J. M. Nouwen; *Abandonment to Divine Providence* by Jean-Pierre De Caussade, copyright © 1975 by John Beevers; *Goethe's Faust*, translated by Walter Kaufmann, copyright © 1961 by Walter Kaufmann; *The Confessions of St. Augustine*, translated by John K. Ryan, copyright © 1960. FORTRESS PRESS: *The Prophetic Imagination* by Walter Brueggemann, copyright © 1978. HARPER & ROW: *The Divine Milieu* by Pierre Teilhard de Chardin, copyright © 1957 by Editions du Seuil, Paris, English language translation copyright © 1960 by Wm. Collins Sons & Co., London, and Harper & Row, Publishers, New York; *Meister Eckhart: A Modern Translation* by Raymond B. Blakney, copyright © 1941. HARVARD UNIVERSITY PRESS: *The Poems of Emily Dickinson*, edited by Thomas H. Johnson, reprinted by permission of the publishers and the Trustees of Amherst College, Cambridge, Mass.: The Belknap Press of Harvard University Press, copyright 1951, © 1955, 1979 by the President and Fellows of Harvard College. HOLT, RINEHART AND WINSTON: *Steppenwolf* by Herman Hesse, copyright © 1963. HOUGHTON MIFFLIN COMPANY: *Apologia pro Vita Sua* by John Henry Cardinal Newman, edited with an introduction and notes by A. Dwight Culler, Riverside Editions No. B10, copyright © 1956 by A. Dwight Culler.

HUTCHINSON & CO., LTD: *Goethe's Faust*, translated by Walter Kaufman, copyright © 1961.

INSTITUTE OF CARMELITE STUDIES: *Story of a Soul: The Autobiography of St. Therese of Lisieux*, translated by John Clarke, O.C.D., copyright © 1975; *The Collected Works of St. John of the Cross*, translated by Kieran Kavanaugh, O.C.D., and Otilio Rodriguez, O.C.D., copyright © 1973.

MACMILLAN PUBLISHING CO., INC.: *Out of the Silent Planet* by C. S. Lewis, copyright © 1965.

DAVID MCKAY CO., INC.: *The Varieties of Religious Experience* by William James, copyright © 1936.

OXFORD UNIVERSITY PRESS: *A Sand County Almanac, with other essays on conservation from Round River* by Aldo Leopold, copyright © 1949, 1953, 1966, renewed 1977, 1981.

PAULIST PRESS: *Julian of Norwich: Showings*, translated and introduction by Edmund Colledge, O.S.A., and James Walsh, S.J., copyright © 1978 by the Missionary Society of St. Paul the Apostle in the State of New York; *Catherine of Siena, The Dialogue*, translated and introduction by Suzanne Noffke, O.P., copyright © 1980 by The Missionary Society of St. Paul the Apostle in the State of New York.

RANDOM HOUSE, INC.: *The Selected Writings of Ralph Waldo Emerson*, edited by Brooks Atkinson, copyright © 1940.

REGNERY GATEWAY: *The Lord* by Romano Guardini, copyright © 1954.

CHARLES SCRIBNER'S SONS: *The Shaking of the Foundations* by Paul Tillich, copyright © 1948; copyright renewed.

SHEED & WARD: *Prayer* by Hans Urs von Balthasar, translated by A. V. Littledale, copyright © 1961.

SIMON & SCHUSTER: *Zorba the Greek* by Nikos Kazantzakis, copyright © 1953, 1981.

PREFACE

Somewhere between the "ought" (ideal) and the "is" (real), hope resides. The dreams that tell us of a world of justice and love must be kept alive; the reality of oppression and indifference must not be denied. Life is a constant striving to move us from the limited experience of everyday life to the fullness of our hopes and desires in the Lord.

This volume of mantras has as its goal to make a contribution to the process of realizing the Lord's truth, goodness, and beauty in our times. Through prayer, here the prayer of the mantra, each individual can keep alive the vision of what can be without denying the shortcomings of the present moment. These meditations draw us into the depth of reality where we meet our God, the source of all life and holiness. In touch with God, we emerge to live what we experience and to share the blessings received. In this living and sharing, the world becomes a little richer and holier.

The Introduction of an earlier volume, *Mantras for the Morning*, is reprinted here to explain to the new reader and to refresh the memory of the veteran the nature of holistic prayer, the process that is continued and expanded in this book.

In recent years many voices in education, business, and medicine have been promoting a holistic approach to the human person. Teachers, they urge, must not only impart information to their students but also help them to integrate their emotions and to act maturely. Thus the cognitive, affective, and behavioral dimensions receive due attention in the education of the whole person. Employers, too, realize that their employees will produce more if they are physically fit and psychologically stable. Some businesses, therefore, provide recreational facilities and counseling services for their workers. Those in the medical field realize that care for the total person will contribute to the restoration or maintenance of good health. They see the patient as much more than a sick body; besides proper physical care, the psychological and spiritual needs of the patient have become concerns in the healing process.

Spiritual growth, too, is a holistic process. It involves all our relationships—with God, with others, with ourselves, and even with nature. Spiritual experiences involve the head, the heart, and the hands. Central to these experiences is prayer, the dialogic process with God. Authentic prayer is not just a head trip or an emotional experience or a moral exercise—it is all these and more. The *whole* person comes to prayer. The stimulus to prayer must be sufficient to allow for the full human participation of the individual or the community.

Prayer is essentially an encounter with God. Ideally, this encounter should elicit a total response from the one praying. Realistically, however, the prayer experience that takes as its stimulus a personal experience, a selection from Scripture, or a meditative reading does not address itself to the whole person but rather to a single dimension of our being: an idea to touch the mind, a song to move the heart, a picture to create a mood, a summary statement to incite an action. In this book we want to provide stimuli for prayer experiences that involve the whole person. When our encounter with God embraces the cognitive, affective, and behavioral aspects of our lives, we will enjoy an integrated spirituality.

Methodology

Twenty-five themes are presented for prayerful reflection. Such themes as healing, hope, kingdom, and conversion are universal. Each theme is encapsulated in a mantra (a phrase or statement of seven syllables to be rhythmically repeated in order to center oneself in prayer or on a single point). The mantra serves as a technique for holding attention, for achieving simplicity in prayer, and for providing unity. As we repeat the mantra reverently and thoughtfully, it becomes a part of our internal timing. Synchronized with our breathing, the mantra resonates at a depth that can touch the very essence of our lives. Furthermore, the mantra helps us to slow down, to journey deep within, to feel the pulse of our inner life, to live from a deeper source. "Through his wounds we are healed," taken from the prophet Isaiah, is such a mantra. To ponder this insight, to feel its movement, to begin to perceive and respond to its truth fosters a new appreciation of God's healing.

The source of these mantras is either Scripture or faith poetry. The mantra is stated and then presented in the more meaningful context of the full biblical reference or poem. This prayer stimulus is then supported by parallel references from the Scriptures that further develop the basic theme and enlarge upon the mantra.

A threefold expansion is then given. A photograph allows us to see experientially how the theme-mantra is found in nature or in human interactions. If indeed a picture is worth many words, then we benefit greatly in using our sight to capture the tone and beauty that escape words. Another advantage is that pictures and images tend to draw us more deeply into life because of their concreteness and familiarity.

A second dimension of the theme-mantra is presented in an appeal to our hearing. Within the verbal silence of the mantra resides a song (more accurately, many songs, depending upon the listeners and the season of one's heart). A single melody, gently extracted from the mantra, allows the power of music to stir the heart and inspire the soul. Deep affectivity resides in music; indeed, all prayer is essentially a song, and the strongest prayer is affective in nature.

The third dimension of the theme-mantra is seen in the written word. The mantra, repeated many times in double lines, journeys into a variety of areas in an attempt to touch concrete human experiences. The intent here is to allow the reader to discover deeper meaning more through poetic intuition than through philosophical reasoning. Images, personalities, and localities are the references offered in order to foster a prayer based more on the particular than on the universal, more on the concrete than on the abstract.

The theme-mantra experienced in its photographic, musical, and verbal dimensions is followed by a short prayer for the grace to live out the theme under consideration. Here the behavioral aspect of spirituality is stressed, and a challenge is presented to our lifestyles. Thus we see the two sides of prayer: the inward journey of being with the Father and the outward thrust of being sent to live the word pondered. Through the visual, auditory, and verbal avenues, the totality of our personality is drawn into the spiritual experience.

Each theme-mantra is then concluded with a series of quotations from various authors: poets, mystics, philosophers, theologians, novelists. In their writings they have articulated some insight that further enriches the theme chosen for prayer. These quotations confirm the significance of the theme and highlight some of its aspects. These quotations in and of themselves might well serve as stimuli for future prayer experiences.

Healing

MANTRA: **Through his wounds we are healed**

SOURCE: Isaiah 53:1–7

"Who could believe what we have heard,
and to whom has the power of Yahweh been revealed?"
Like a sapling he grew up in front of us,
like a root in arid ground.
Without beauty, without majesty (we saw him),
no looks to attract our eyes;
a thing despised and rejected by men,
a man of sorrows and familiar with suffering,
a man to make people screen their faces;
he was despised and we took no account of him.

And yet ours were the sufferings he bore,
ours the sorrows he carried.
But we, we thought of him as someone punished,
struck by God, and brought low.
Yet he was pierced through for our faults,
crushed for our sins.
On him lies a punishment that brings us peace,
and through his wounds we are healed.

We had all gone astray like sheep,
each taking his own way,
and Yahweh burdened him
with the sins of all of us.
Harshly dealt with, he bore it humbly,
he never opened his mouth,
like a lamb that is led to the slaughterhouse,
like a sheep that is dumb before its shearers
never opening its mouth.

12

PARALLEL REFERENCES

This, in fact, is what you were called to do, because Christ suffered for you and left an example for you to follow the way he took. He had not done anything wrong, and there had been no perjury in his mouth. He was insulted and did not retaliate with insults; when he was tortured he made no threats but he put his trust in the righteous judge. He was bearing our faults in his body on the cross, so that we might die to our faults and live for holiness; through his wounds you have been healed. You had gone astray like sheep but now you have come back to the shepherd and guardian of your souls. (*1 Peter 2:21-24*)

For our sake God made the sinless one into sin, so that in him we might become the goodness of God. (*2 Corinthians 5:21*)

Through his wounds we are healed.

THE DOCTOR

THROUGH HIS WOUNDS WE ARE HEALED,
THROUGH HIS WOUNDS WE ARE HEALED.
> Your hands, Lord, pierced by crude and cruel nails,
> Your feet, Lord, torn by blunt and brutal iron,
> Your side, Lord, scalpeled by an unwitting spear.

THROUGH HIS WOUNDS WE ARE HEALED,
THROUGH HIS WOUNDS WE ARE HEALED.
> Healing our insensitive and grasping fingers,
> Healing our wandering and delinquent steps,
> Healing our indulged and golden-calf bellies.

THROUGH HIS WOUNDS WE ARE HEALED,
THROUGH HIS WOUNDS WE ARE HEALED.
> Your mind, Lord, abused with our lies and deceptions,
> Your heart, Lord, exploited by our avarice and pride,
> Your spirit, Lord, mocked and ridiculed by our sin.

THROUGH HIS WOUNDS WE ARE HEALED,
THROUGH HIS WOUNDS WE ARE HEALED.
> Healing our thoughts with truth and wisdom,
> Healing our hearts with joy and warmth,
> Healing our spirit with grace and hope.

PRAYER

Lord, we come before you in our illness, longing for your gentle touch and loving embrace. Your wounded body and spirit heal us; your brokenness restores us to wholeness. Praise to you, our God, for your mercy and kindness.

QUOTATIONS FROM HENRI NOUWEN*

We are all healers who can reach out to
offer health, and we all are patients in
constant need of help. Only this realization
can keep professionals from becoming distant
technicians and those in need of care from
feeling used or manipulated.

But when we look at healing as creating space
for the stranger, it is clear that all Christians
should be willing and able to offer this so
much needed form of hospitality.

Therefore, healing means, first of all, the
creation of an empty but friendly space where
those who suffer can tell their story to someone who can listen with real attention.

Our most important question as healers is not,
"What to say or to do?" but, "How to develop
enough inner space where the story can be
received?" Healing is the humble but also very
demanding task of creating and offering a friendly
empty space where strangers can reflect on their
pain and suffering without fear, and find the confidence that makes them look for new ways right in
the center of their confusion.

*Henri J. M. Nouwen, *Reaching Out: The Three Movements of the Spiritual
Life* (New York: Doubleday and Company, Inc., 1975) 65, 66, 67, 68.

Forgiveness

MANTRA: **With your love remember me**

SOURCE: Psalm 25:1-11

To you, Yahweh, I lift up my soul,
O my God.

I rely on you, do not let me be shamed,
do not let my enemies gloat over me!
No, those who hope in you are never shamed,
shame awaits disappointed traitors.

Yahweh, make your ways known to me,
teach me your paths.
Set me in the way of your truth, and teach me,
for you are the God who saves me.

All day long I hope in you
because of your goodness, Yahweh.
Remember your kindness, Yahweh,
your love, that you showed long ago.
Do not remember the sins of my youth;
but rather, with your love remember me.

Yahweh is so good, so upright,
he teaches the way to sinners;
in all that is right he guides the humble,
and instructs the poor in his way.

All Yahweh's paths are love and truth
for those who keep his covenant and his decrees.
For the sake of your name, Yahweh,
forgive my guilt, for it is great.

PARALLEL REFERENCES

One of the criminals hanging there abused him. "Are you the Christ?"
he said. "Save yourself and us as well." But the other spoke up and
rebuked him. "Have you no fear of God at all?" he said. "You got
the same sentence as he did, but in our case we deserved it: we are
paying for what we did. But this man has done nothing wrong.
Jesus," he said "remember me when you come into your kingdom."
"Indeed, I promise you," he replied, "today you will be with me in
paradise." *(Luke 23:39-43)*

Do not let your anger go too far, Yahweh,
or go on thinking of our sins for ever. *(Isaiah 64:8)*

With your love re-mem-ber me.

INNER TREASURY

Do not remember the stolen pears and haughty eyebrows,
Do not remember the half truths and mocking gossip,
Do not remember the cup withheld and hospitality neglected,
   WITH YOUR LOVE REMEMBER ME,
   WITH YOUR LOVE REMEMBER ME.

Do not remember the wasted time and roads not taken,
Do not remember the strident word and hellbound silence,
Do not remember principles forsaken and friends abandoned,
   WITH YOUR LOVE REMEMBER ME,
   WITH YOUR LOVE REMEMBER ME.

Do not remember the confidence broken and trust betrayed,
Do not remember gifts discarded and seeds unplanted,
Do not remember songs unsung and poems unwritten,
   WITH YOUR LOVE REMEMBER ME,
   WITH YOUR LOVE REMEMBER ME.

PRAYER

Lord, your memory is powerful and clear. Remember not the sins
of our youth, the broken lives of our mid-years, the offenses of old
age. Remember not our insensitivity and pride. Remember only
our responses to your grace. May we praise you forever. Amen.

QUOTATIONS FROM JOHN PAUL II*

Society can become "ever more human" only when we introduce into all the mutual relationships that form its moral aspect the moment of forgiveness, which is so much of the essence of the Gospel. Forgiveness demonstrates the presence in the world of the love that is more powerful than sin. Forgiveness is also the fundamental condition for reconciliation, not only in the relationship of God with humanity, but also in relationships between people. A world from which forgiveness was eliminated would be nothing but a world of cold and unfeeling justice, in the name of which each person would claim his or her own rights vis-à-vis others; the various kinds of selfishness latent in people would transform life and human society into a system of oppression of the weak by the strong, or into an arena of permanent strife between one group and another.

Christ emphasizes so insistently the need to forgive others that when Peter asked him how many times he should forgive his neighbor he answered with the symbolic number of "seventy times seven," meaning that he must be able to forgive everyone every time. It is obvious that such a generous requirement of forgiveness does not cancel out the objective requirements of justice. Properly understood, justice constitutes, so to speak, the goal of forgiveness. In no passage of the Gospel message does forgiveness, or mercy as its source, mean indulgence towards evil, towards scandals, towards injury or insult. In any case, reparation for evil and scandal, compensation for injury, and satisfaction for insult are conditions for forgiveness.

The Church must consider it one of her principal duties—at every stage of history and especially in our modern age—to proclaim and to introduce into life the mystery of mercy, supremely revealed in Jesus Christ. Not only for the Church herself as the community of believers but also in a certain sense for all people, this mystery is the source of a life different from the life that can be built by those who are exposed to the oppressive forces of the threefold concupiscence active within them. It is precisely in the name of this mystery that Christ teaches us to forgive always.

*Encyclical Letter *Dives in Misericordia* of Pope John Paul II, November 30, 1980, #14.

Fear

MANTRA: **Down the nights and down the days**

SOURCE: Francis Thompson, "The Hound of Heaven"

I fled Him, down the nights and down the days;
   I fled Him, down the arches of the years;
I fled Him, down the labyrinthine ways
    Of my own mind; and in the midst of tears
I hid from Him, and under running laughter.
      Up vistaed hopes I sped;
      And shot, precipitated,
Adown Titanic glooms of chasmèd fears,
    From those strong Feet that followed, followed after.
     But with unhurrying chase,
     And unperturbèd pace,
Deliberate speed, majestic instancy,
    They beat—and a Voice beat
    More instant than the Feet—
"All things betray thee, who betrayest Me."

PARALLEL REFERENCES

Meanwhile Saul was still breathing threats to slaughter the Lord's disciples. He had gone to the high priest and asked for letters addressed to the synagogues in Damascus, that would authorize him to arrest and take to Jerusalem any followers of the Way, men or women, that he could find.

Suddenly, while he was travelling to Damascus and just before he reached the city, there came a light from heaven all around him. He fell to the ground, and then he heard a voice saying, "Saul, Saul, why are you persecuting me?" (*Acts 9:1-4*)

All the time I kept silent, my bones were wasting away
with groans, day in, day out;
day and night your hand
lay heavy on me;
my heart grew parched as stubble
in summer drought.

At last I admitted to you I had sinned;
no longer concealing my guilt,
I said, "I will go to Yahweh
and confess my fault."
And you, you have forgiven the wrong I did,
have pardoned my sin. (*Psalm 32:3-5*)

Down the nights and down the days.

THE FLIGHT

I ran with the wind,
   I fell deep into sin,
       DOWN THE NIGHTS AND DOWN THE DAYS,
       DOWN THE NIGHTS AND DOWN THE DAYS.

I circled my fears,
   I forced back my tears,
       DOWN THE NIGHTS AND DOWN THE DAYS,
       DOWN THE NIGHTS AND DOWN THE DAYS.

I flew from all love,
   I moaned like a dove,
       DOWN THE NIGHTS AND DOWN THE DAYS,
       DOWN THE NIGHTS AND DOWN THE DAYS.

I hid from the stars,
   I stood behind bars,
       DOWN THE NIGHTS AND DOWN THE DAYS,
       DOWN THE NIGHTS AND DOWN THE DAYS.

I concealed my flaws,
   I fled freedom's laws,
       DOWN THE NIGHTS AND DOWN THE DAYS,
       DOWN THE NIGHTS AND DOWN THE DAYS.

Down the nights and down the days.

PRAYER

Gracious Lord, you pursue us with tenderness and mercy. Why do
we flee from your love; why do we fear your embrace? Help us to
see your glory. Then it will be we who pursue you down the nights
and down the days, throughout all the seasons of our lives. Come,
Lord, come.

QUOTATIONS FROM JOHN HENRY NEWMAN*

My difficulty was this: I had been deceived greatly once; how could I be sure that I was not deceived a second time?

To consider the world in its length and breadth, its various history, the many races of man, their starts, their fortunes, their mutual alienation, their conflicts; and then their ways, habits, governments, forms of worship; their enterprises, their aimless courses, their random achievements and acquirements, the impotent conclusion of long-standing facts, the tokens so faint and broken of superintending design, the blind evolution of what turn out to be great powers of truths, the progress of things, as if from unreasoning elements, not towards final causes, the greatness and littleness of man, his far-reaching aims, his short duration, the curtain hung over his futurity, the disappointments of life, the defeat of good, the success of evil, physical pain, mental anguish, the prevalence and intensity of sin, the pervading idolatries, the corruptions, the dreary hopeless irreligion, that condition of the whole race, so fearfully yet exactly described in the Apostle's words, "having no hope and without God in the world,"—all this is a vision to dizzy and appall; and inflicts upon the mind and the sense a profound mystery, which is absolutely beyond human solution.

The energy of the human intellect 'does from opposition grow'; it thrives and is joyous, with a tough elastic strength, under the terrible blows of the divinely fashioned weapon, and is never so much itself as when it has lately been overthrown.

*John Henry Newman, *Apologia pro Vita Sua* (Boston: The Riverside Press Cambridge, 1965) 217, 230, 238.

Memory

MANTRA: **I am the one forgot thee**

SOURCE: Emily Dickinson

Savior! I've no one else to tell—
And so I trouble thee.
I am the one forgot thee so—
Dost thou remember me?
Nor, for myself, I came so far—
That were the little load—
I brought thee the imperial Heart
I had not strength to hold—
The Heart I carried in my own—
Till mine too heavy grew—
Yet—strangest—heavier since it went—
Is it too large for you?

PARALLEL REFERENCES

Have mercy on me, O God, in your goodness,
in your great tenderness wipe away my faults;
wash me clean of my guilt,
purify me from my sin.

For I am well aware of my faults,
I have my sin constantly in mind,
having sinned against none other than you,
having done what you regard as wrong. (*Psalm 51:1-4*)

"Jerusalem, Jerusalem, you that kill the prophets and stone those
who are sent to you! How often have I longed to gather your children, as a hen gathers her brood under her wings, and you refused!
So be it! Your house will be left to you. Yes, I promise you, you
shall not see me till the time comes when you say: Blessings on him
who comes in the name of the Lord!" (*Luke 13:34-35*)

I am the one for-got thee.

FORGET-ME-NOTS

I AM THE ONE FORGOT THEE,
I AM THE ONE FORGOT THEE,
on summer days preoccupied with play,
in meetings devoid of meaning,
at intersections replete with confusion.

I AM THE ONE FORGOT THEE,
I AM THE ONE FORGOT THEE,
on winter eves covered with frost,
in close encounters breaking hearts and hearths,
at crises needing light.

I AM THE ONE FORGOT THEE,
I AM THE ONE FORGOT THEE,
on autumn hills exuding death,
in conversations begun in haste,
at passages filled with fears.

I AM THE ONE FORGOT THEE,
I AM THE ONE FORGOT THEE,
on spring morns revealing your glory, the divine story,
in whispers voicing so gently your mercy, endless mercy,
at crossroads dividing the courageous and the coward.

I am the one for-got thee.

PRAYER

Lord, too often I fail to live in your presence. The seasons come
and go, people enter my life and are too quickly forgotten, decisions
responding to your call long delayed. I fail to turn to you for help
and support. Grant me the peace to remember your love and compassion—to always trust in your ways.

QUOTATIONS FROM C. S. LEWIS*

. . . then he begets young; then he rears them; then he remembers all this, and boils it inside him and makes it into poems and wisdom.

"A pleasure is full grown only when it is remembered. You are speaking, Hman, as if the pleasure were one thing and the memory another. It is all one thing. The seroni could say it better than I say it now. Not better than I could say it in a poem. What you call remembering is the last part of the pleasure, as the crah is the last part of a poem. When you and I met, the meeting was over very shortly, it was nothing. Now it is growing something as we remember it. But still we know very little about it. What it will be when I remember it as I lie down to die, what it makes me all my days till then—that is the real meeting. The other is only the beginning of it. You say you have poets in your world. Do they teach you this?"

I will tell you a day in my life that has shaped me.

. . . but he gathered that books were few in Malacandra. "It is better to remember," said the sorns.

*C. S. Lewis, *Out of the Silent Planet* (New York: The Macmillan Company, 1965) 73, 75, 101.

Peace

MANTRA: **An instrument of your peace**

SOURCE: Prayer of St. Francis of Assisi

Lord, make me an instrument of your peace.
Where there is hatred, let me sow love;
where there is injury, pardon;
where there is doubt, faith;
where there is despair, hope;
where there is darkness, light;
and where there is sadness, joy.

O Divine Master, grant that I may not so much seek
to be consoled as to console;
to be understood as to understand;
to be loved as to love;
for it is in giving that we receive;
it is in pardoning that we are pardoned;
and it is in dying that we are born to eternal life.

PARALLEL REFERENCES

For anyone who is in Christ, there is a new creation; the old creation
has gone, and now the new one is here. It is all God's work. It was
God who reconciled us to himself through Christ and gave us the
work of handing on this reconciliation. In other words, God in
Christ was reconciling the world to himself, not holding men's
faults against them, and he has entrusted to us the news that they
are reconciled. So we are ambassadors for Christ; it is as though
God were appealing through us, and the appeal that we make in
Christ's name is: be reconciled to God. (*2 Corinthians 5:17-20*)

"Whatever town or village you go into, ask for someone trustworthy and stay with him until you leave. As you enter his house, salute it, and if the house deserves it, let your peace descend upon it; if it does not, let your peace come back to you. And if anyone does not welcome you or listen to what you have to say, as you walk out of the house or town shake the dust from your feet. I tell you solemnly, on the day of Judgment it will not go as hard with the land of Sodom and Gomorrah as with that town. Remember, I am sending you out like sheep among wolves; so be cunning as serpents and yet as harmless as doves." (*Matthew 10:11-16*)

An in-stru-ment of your peace.

THE CRAFTSMAN

Lord, you made the bell to proclaim your love,
    you made the pen to spell the message of good news,
    you made morning light to vanquish dark fears,
    so now make me
           AN INSTRUMENT OF YOUR PEACE,
           AN INSTRUMENT OF YOUR PEACE.

Lord, you made the knife to still our hunger,
    you made a joke to tickle the rib of Adam,
    you made the snail to forestall our hurriedness,
    so now make me
           AN INSTRUMENT OF YOUR PEACE,
           AN INSTRUMENT OF YOUR PEACE.

Lord, you made the needle to mend broken hearts,
    you made the raven to whisper a haunting nevermore,
    you made the lemon to tempt the sweet with bitter,
    so now make me
           AN INSTRUMENT OF YOUR PEACE,
           AN INSTRUMENT OF YOUR PEACE.

Lord, you made the hill to gentle our solitude,
    you made the river to flow with richness of life,
    you made the desert to measure our finitude,
    so now make me
           AN INSTRUMENT OF YOUR PEACE,
           AN INSTRUMENT OF YOUR PEACE.

An in-stru-ment of your peace.

PRAYER

Lord, creative and loving Father, you make all things new. All creation is a channel and instrument of your richness and bounty. Form me into a fitting channel of your grace; mold me into a worthy instrument of your love. Grant this in the name of Jesus the Christ.

QUOTATIONS FROM POPE JOHN XXIII*

Peace on earth, which people of every era have most eagerly yearned for, can be firmly established only if the order laid down by God is dutifully observed.

The fundamental principle on which our present peace depends must be replaced by another, which declares that the true and solid peace of nations can consist, not in equality of arms, but in mutual trust alone.

There can be no peace between people unless there is peace within each one of them, unless, that is, each one builds up within oneself the order wished by God.

Peace will be but an empty-sounding word unless it is founded on the order that this present document has outlined in confident hope: an order founded on truth, built according to justice, vivified and integrated by charity, and put into practice in freedom.

*Encyclical Letter *Pacem in Terris* of Pope John XXIII, April 11, 1963, #1, 113, 165, 167.

Perfection

MANTRA: **What more do I need to do?**

SOURCE: Matthew 19:16–22

There was a man who came to him and asked, "Master, what good deed must I do to possess eternal life?" Jesus said to him, "Why do you ask me about what is good? There is one alone who is good. But if you wish to enter into life, keep the commandments." He said, "Which?" "These": Jesus replied, "You must not kill. You must not commit adultery. You must not steal. You must not bring false witness. Honor your father and mother, and: you must love your neighbor as yourself." The young man said to him, "I have kept all these. What more do I need to do?" Jesus said, "If you wish to be perfect, go and sell what you own and give the money to the poor, and you will have treasure in heaven; then come, follow me." But when the young man heard these words he went away sad, for he was a man of great wealth.

PARALLEL REFERENCES

It happened some time later that God put Abraham to the test. "Abraham, Abraham," he called. "Here I am," he replied. "Take your son," God said, "your only child Isaac, whom you love, and go to the land of Moriah. There you shall offer him as a burnt offering, on a mountain I will point out to you." (*Genesis 22:1-2*)

All I want is to know Christ and the power of his resurrection and to share his sufferings by reproducing the pattern of his death. That is the way I can hope to take my place in the resurrection of the dead. Not that I have become perfect yet: I have not yet won, but I am still running, trying to capture the prize for which Christ Jesus captured me. (*Philippians 3:10-13*)

What more do I need to do?

LEGAL MORENESS

WHAT MORE DO I NEED TO DO?
WHAT MORE DO I NEED TO DO?

> I have not destroyed — man nor beast!
>
> I have not betrayed friendships — in deed or thought!
>
> I have not lied — whether convenient or inconvenient!
>
> I have not dishonored — those who gave me life!
>
> I have not neglected — fellow pilgrim or my own heart!
>
> I have not . . .

WHAT MORE DO I NEED TO DO?
WHAT MORE DO I NEED TO DO?

> Perhaps I am to pray three hours a day!
>
> Perhaps I am to make heroic sacrifices!
>
> Perhaps I am to fast several times a week!
>
> Perhaps I am to be all things to all people!
>
> Perhaps I am to not be . . . but die!
>
> Perhaps . . .

WHAT MORE DO I NEED TO DO?
WHAT MORE DO I NEED TO DO?

GO   SELL   GIVE
THEN
COME, FOLLOW ME

What more do I need to do?

PRAYER

Lord, I am confused. What indeed am I to do with my limited life and gifts? Help me to discern your voice as you call me to your loving plan. May my life give you fitting praise and honor. Amen.

QUOTATIONS FROM ST. THERESE OF LISIEUX*

And so it is in the world of souls, Jesus' garden. He willed to create great souls comparable to lilies and roses, but He has created smaller ones and these must be content to be daisies or violets destined to give joy to God's glances when He looks down at His feet. Perfection consists in doing His will, in being what He wills us to be.

This little incident of my childhood is a summary of my whole life; later on when perfection was set before me, I understood that to become a saint one had to suffer much, seek out always the most perfect thing to do, and forget self. I understood, too, there were many degrees of perfection and each soul was free to respond to the advances of Our Lord, to do little or much for Him in a word, to choose among the sacrifices He was asking. Then, as in the days of my childhood, I cried out: "My God 'I choose all!' I don't want to be a saint by halves, I'm not afraid to suffer for You, I fear only one thing: to keep my own will; so take it, for 'I choose all' that You will!"

But soon God made me feel that true glory is that which will last eternally, and to reach it, it isn't necessary to perform striking works but to hide oneself and practice virtue in such a way that the left hand knows not what the right is doing.

Because I was little and weak He lowered Himself to me, and He instructed me secretly in the things of His love. Ah! had the learned who spent their life in study come to me, undoubtedly they would have been astonished to see a child of fourteen understand perfection's secrets, secrets all their knowledge cannot reveal because to possess them one has to be poor in spirit!

I see that suffering alone gives birth to souls.

*Story of a Soul: The Autobiography of St. Therese of Lisieux, trans. John Clarke, O.C.D. (Washington, D.C.: ICS Publications - Institute of Carmelite Studies, 1975) 14, 27, 72, 105, 174.

Obedience

MANTRA: **He did as Yahweh had said**

SOURCE: 1 Kings 17:1-6

Elijah the Tishbite, of Tishbe in Gilead, said to Ahab, "As Yahweh lives, the God of Israel whom I serve, there shall be neither dew nor rain these years except at my order."
The word of Yahweh came to him, "Go away from here, go eastwards, and hide yourself in the wadi Cherith which lies east of Jordan. You can drink from the stream, and I have ordered the ravens to bring you food there." He did as Yahweh had said; he went and stayed in the wadi Cherith which lies east of Jordan. The ravens brought him bread in the morning and meat in the evening, and he quenched his thirst at the stream.

PARALLEL REFERENCES

Then Moses said to God, "I am to go, then, to the sons of Israel and say to them, 'The God of your fathers has sent me to you.' But if they ask me what his name is, what am I to tell them?" And God said to Moses, "I Am who I Am. This," he added, "is what you must say to the sons of Israel: 'I Am has sent me to you.'" And God also said to Moses, "You are to say to the sons of Israel: 'Yahweh, the God of your fathers, the God of Abraham, the God of Isaac, and the God of Jacob, has sent me to you.' This is my name for all time; by this name I shall be invoked for all generations to come." (*Exodus 3:13-15*)

In the fifteenth year of Tiberius Caesar's reign, when Pontius Pilate was governor of Judaea, Herod tetrarch of Galilee, his brother Philip tetrarch of the lands of Ituraea and Trachonitis, Lysanias tetrarch of Abilene, during the pontificate of Annas and Caiaphas, the word of God came to John son of Zechariah, in the wilderness. He went through the whole Jordan district proclaiming a baptism of repentance for the forgiveness of sins. (*Luke 3:1-3*)

He did as Yah-weh had said.

He did as Yah-weh had said.

LISTENING

HE DID AS YAHWEH HAD SAID,
HE DID AS YAHWEH HAD SAID.
>Jesus did . . . and love became enfleshed,
>Jesus did . . . and sin lost its power,
>Jesus did . . . and death's sting was no more.

HE DID AS YAHWEH HAD SAID,
HE DID AS YAHWEH HAD SAID.
>Peter did . . . and the Church found a rock,
>John did . . . and Mary gained a son,
>Paul did . . . and the Gentiles discovered hope.

HE DID AS YAHWEH HAD SAID,
HE DID AS YAHWEH HAD SAID.
>Augustine did . . . a community flowered forth,
>Francis did . . . a new song of poverty pierced the world,
>Catherine did . . . a new order was born.

HE DID AS YAHWEH HAD SAID,
HE DID AS YAHWEH HAD SAID.
>Judas did not . . . and death filled the garden,
>The rich young man did not . . . and his face fell,
>The crowd did not . . . and they hunger still.

PRAYER

Lord, grant us the gift of obedience. May we hear your voice, sense your touch, see your marvelous deeds. And when we know what you ask of us, empower us to do your truth in love. We praise you for your call; we thank you for your power—for we are your people and servants, you are our God and Lord. Amen.

QUOTATIONS FROM JEAN-PIERRE DE CAUSSADE*

In reality, holiness consists of one thing only: complete loyalty to God's will.

If we carefully fulfill the duties imposed on us by our state of life, if we quietly follow any impulse coming from God, if we peacefully submit to the influence of grace, we are making an act of total abandonment.

When he finds them pure and free of all reserve, he fills them with himself, for, being emptied of all things, our hearts have an infinite capacity and so are able to receive him. O holy detachment! It is you who makes room for God! O purity! O complete surrender! It is you who draw God into my heart!

All he wants from us is an honest, straight-forward, simple, submissive and loyal heart. When he finds such a heart, he takes possession of it, controls all its responses, and so uses it that it finds in everything, no matter what, something which is invaluable in its progress to holiness.

*Jean-Pierre De Caussade, *Abandonment to Divine Providence* (New York: Doubleday & Company, 1975) 24, 66, 113.

Courage

MANTRA: **The mastery of the thing**

SOURCE: Gerard Manley Hopkins, "The Windhover: To Christ our Lord"

I caught this morning morning's minion, king-
  dom of daylight's dauphin, dapple-dawn-drawn Falcon,
      in his riding
Of the rolling level underneath him steady air, and striding
High there, how he rung upon the rein of a wimpling wing
In his ecstasy! then off, off forth on swing,
  As a skate's heel sweeps smooth on a bow-bend:
      the hurl and gliding
  Rebuffed the big wind. My heart in hiding
Stirred for a bird, the achieve of, the mastery of the thing!

Brute beauty and valour and act, oh, air, pride, plume here
  Buckle! and the fire that breaks from thee then, a billion
Times told lovelier, more dangerous, O my chevalier!

No wonder of it: sheer plod makes plough down sillion
Shine, and blue-bleak embers, ah my dear,
  Fall, gall themselves, and gash gold-vermilion.

PARALLEL REFERENCE

Stephen, filled with the Holy Spirit, gazed into heaven and saw
the glory of God, and Jesus standing at God's right hand. "I can see
heaven thrown open," he said, "and the Son of Man standing at
the right hand of God." At this all the members of the council
shouted out and stopped their ears with their hands; then they all
rushed at him, sent him out of the city and stoned him. The witnesses
put down their clothes at the feet of a young man called Saul. As
they were stoning him, Stephen said in invocation, "Lord Jesus,
receive my spirit." Then he knelt down and said aloud, "Lord, do
not hold this sin against them"; and with these words he fell asleep.
(*Acts 7:55-60*)

The mas - ter - y of the thing.

THOSE WHO DARED

> THE MASTERY OF THE THING,
> THE MASTERY OF THE THING.

delicate gossamer: a sketch of the cosmos!
crystal snowflake: frozen masterpiece of divine artistry!
child's tear: sparkling diamond of human pain!

> THE MASTERY OF THE THING,
> THE MASTERY OF THE THING.

surgeon's hands: healing care in slow motion!
teacher's word: eloquent music of gracious insight!
mother's touch: gentle caress of heart's concern!

> THE MASTERY OF THE THING,
> THE MASTERY OF THE THING.

rabbit's ear: soft velvet at proud attention!
kitten's paw: mysterious identity from cautious footprints!
cardinal's song: thrilling sound of ecstatic melody!

> THE MASTERY OF THE THING,
> THE MASTERY OF THE THING.

towering skyscraper: soaring temple of technical ingenuity!
northern igloo: creative sculpture in ice and snow!
extravagant galaxy: swirling stars of incomprehensible beauty!

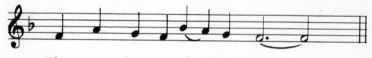

The mas-ter-y of the thing.

PRAYER

God, creator of the universe, mastery of all life, you thrill us with
your divine pluralism. Fill us all with reverence for your handiwork;
teach us to see your presence in every atom. What mastery we find
in the flight of a hawk, in the petal of a flower, in the voice of a friend.
Herein we find you, our maker and lord. Praise and honor be yours
forever.

QUOTATIONS FROM ALDO LEOPOLD*

The saw works only across the years, which it must deal with one by one, in sequence. From each year the raker teeth pull little chips of fact, which accumulate in little piles, called sawdust by woodsmen and archives by historians; both judge the character of what lies within by the character of the samples thus made visible without. It is not until the transect is completed that the tree falls, and the stump yields a collective view of a century. By its fall the tree attests the unity of the hodge-podge called history.

There are degrees and kinds of solitude. An island in a lake has one kind; but lakes have boats, and there is always the chance that one might land to pay you a visit. A peak in the clouds has another kind; but most peaks have trails, and trails have tourists. I know of no solitude so secure as one guarded by a spring flood; nor do the geese, who have seen more kinds and degrees of aloneness than I have.

This song of the waters is audible to every ear, but there is other music in these hills, by no means audible to all. To hear even a few notes of it you must first live here for a long time, and you must know the speech of hills and rivers. Then on a still night, when the campfire is low and the Pleiades have climbed over rimrocks, sit quietly and listen for a wolf to howl, and think hard of everything you have seen and tried to understand. Then you may hear it—a vast pulsing harmony—its score inscribed on a thousand hills, its notes the lives and deaths of plants and animals, its rhythms spanning the seconds and the centuries.

*Aldo Leopold, *A Sand County Almanac*, illus. Charles W. Schwartz (New York: Ballantine Books, Inc., 1966) 18, 27, 158.

Love

MANTRA: **Learn to bear the beams of love**

SOURCE: William Blake, "The Little Black Boy"

My mother bore me in the southern wild,
And I am black, but O! my soul is white;
White as an angel is the English child,
But I am black, as if bereaved of light.

My mother taught me underneath a tree,
And, sitting down before the heat of day,
She took me on her lap and kissed me,
And, pointing to the east, began to say:

"Look on the rising sun—there God does live,
And gives His light, and gives His heat away;
And flowers and trees and beasts and men receive
Comfort in morning, joy in the noonday.

"And we are put on earth a little space,
That we may learn to bear the beams of love,
And these black bodies and this sunburnt face
Is but a cloud, and like a shady grove.

"For when our souls have learned the heat to bear,
The cloud will vanish; we shall hear His voice,
Saying: 'Come out from the grove, My love and care,
And round My golden tent like lambs rejoice.'"

Thus did my mother say, and kissed me;
And thus I say to little English boy.
When I from black and he from white cloud free,
And round the tent of God like lambs we joy,

I'll shade him from the heat, till he can bear
To lean in joy upon our Father's knee;
And then I'll stand and stroke his silver hair,
And be like him, and he will then love me.

PARALLEL REFERENCES

And he (the rich young man) said to him (Jesus), "Master, I have kept all these from my earliest days." Jesus looked steadily at him and loved him, and he said, "There is one thing you lack. Go and sell everything you own and give the money to the poor, and you will have treasure in heaven; then come, follow me." But his face fell at these words and he went away sad, for he was a man of great wealth. (*Mark 10:20-22*)

Because you are precious in my eyes,
because you are honored and I love you,
I give men in exchange for you,
peoples in return for your life.
Do not be afraid, for I am with you. (*Isaiah 43:4-5*)

Learn to bear the beams of love.

A LESSON

LEARN TO BEAR THE BEAMS OF LOVE,
LEARN TO BEAR THE BEAMS OF LOVE.
    do not hide within groves of sin and darkness,
    do not let clouds of fear block my burning gaze,
    do not shield your body from my tender touch.

LEARN TO BEAR THE BEAMS OF LOVE,
LEARN TO BEAR THE BEAMS OF LOVE.
    in the morning time catch the beams of my dawning comfort,
    in the noon time bravely welcome my piercing joy,
    in the evening time embrace the precious gem of my presence.

LEARN TO BEAR THE BEAMS OF LOVE,
LEARN TO BEAR THE BEAMS OF LOVE.
    through the kiss of a mother/friend, you are beloved,
    through the rising sun/moon, you are beheld,
    through the gifts of light/heat, you are begotten.

LEARN TO BEAR THE BEAMS OF LOVE,
LEARN TO BEAR THE BEAMS OF LOVE.
    regardless of costly tears and midnight fears,
    despite painful joys and broken toys,
    notwithstanding rainy days and flowerless Mays.

PRAYER

Father, your love is beyond measure and your mercy knows no limits. Guide us to the knowledge of your love and grant us the courage to stand in your presence with reverence and awe. May no person refuse your gentle and tender embrace. Father, may your gaze shine on us and fill us with your grace. We ask this through Jesus the Lord. Amen.

QUOTATIONS FROM ST. JOHN OF THE CROSS*

Love effects a likeness between the lover and the object loved.

Nothing is obtained from God except by love.

True love receives all things that come from the Beloved—prosperity, adversity, even chastisement—with the same evenness of soul, since they are his will.

Love produces such likeness in this transformation of lovers that one can say each is the other and both are one. The reason is, that in the union and transformation of love each gives possession of self to the other, and each leaves and exchanges self for the other.

Hence it is that even though a soul may have the highest knowledge and contemplation of God and know all mysteries, yet if it does not love, this knowledge will be of no avail to her union with God.

It is worthy of note that God does not place his grace and love in the soul except according to its desire and love.

The Collected Works of St. John of the Cross, trans. Kieran Kavanaugh, O.C.D., and Otilio Rodriquez, O.C.D. (ICS Publications. Institute of Carmelite Studies, Washington, D.C., 1973) 78, 421, 455, 461, 462.

Trust

MANTRA: **I am a link in a chain**

SOURCE: Prayer by John Henry Newman

God has created me to do him some definite service; he has committed some work to me which he has not committed to another. I have my mission—I may never know it in this life, but I shall be told it in the next.

I am a link in a chain, a bond of connection between persons. He has not created me for naught. I shall do good, I shall do his work. I shall be an angel of peace, a preacher of truth in my own place while not intending it—if I do but keep his commandments.

Therefore I will trust him. Whatever, wherever I am, I can never be thrown away. If I am in sickness, my sickness may serve him; in perplexity, my perplexity may serve him; if I am in sorrow, my sorrow may serve him. He does nothing in vain. He knows what he is about. He may take away my friends. He may throw me among strangers. He may make me feel desolate, make my spirits sink, hide my future from me—still he knows what he is about.

PARALLEL REFERENCES

Trust in Yahweh and do what is good,
make your home in the land and live in peace;
make Yahweh your only joy
and he will give you what your heart desires.

Commit your fate to Yahweh,
trust in him and he will act:
making your virtue clear as the light,
your integrity as bright as noon.

Be quiet before Yahweh, and wait patiently for him. (*Psalm 37:3-7*)

Now John in his prison had heard what Christ was doing and he sent his disciples to ask him, "Are you the one who is to come, or have we got to wait for someone else?" Jesus answered, "Go back and tell John what you hear and see; the blind see again, and the lame walk, lepers are cleansed, and the deaf hear, the dead are raised to life and the Good News is proclaimed to the poor; and happy is the man who does not lose faith in me." (*Matthew 11:2-5*)

I am a link in a chain.

THE DIVINE BLACKSMITH

I AM A LINK IN A CHAIN,
I AM A LINK IN A CHAIN.
    the divine forge aglow with blazing heat,
    the shining anvil awaiting red hot iron,
    the poised hammer raised to mold yet another link.

I AM A LINK IN A CHAIN,
I AM A LINK IN A CHAIN.
    the blacksmith divine sees far beyond the moment,
    the pile of unyielding iron frightened at his glance,
    the needy world longing for the bonding power of love.

I AM A LINK IN A CHAIN,
I AM A LINK IN A CHAIN.
    and so the chain was formed:
        Paul—linking Gentile and Jew,
        Augustine—linking senses and spirit,
        Aquinas—linking reason and faith,

        Thomas More—linking politics and religion,
        Catherine of Siena—linking holiness and service,
        Ignatius—linking contemplation and ministry,
        Newman—linking learning and simplicity.

I AM A LINK IN A CHAIN,
I AM A LINK IN A CHAIN.
    I too am called to foster oneness and peace,
    to reconcile all that is fragmented,
    to be part of a master plan of love.

I am a link in a chain.

PRAYER

Gracious Father, you shape and mold our lives in powerful and gentle ways. Help us to realize our role in the plan of salvation; help us to see that we are a link in the chain of your masterful design. Often we are confused. Our role in life is ambiguous. Grant us the grace to trust in your ways.

QUOTATIONS FROM JULIAN OF NORWICH*

The third (thing) is that we have great trust in him, out of complete and true faith, for it is his will that we know that he will appear, suddenly and blessedly, to all his lovers. For he works in secret, and he will be perceived, and his appearing will be very sudden. And he wants to be trusted, for he is very accessible, familiar and courteous, blessed may he be.

You will see yourself that every kind of thing will be well, as if he said: Accept it now in faith and trust, and in the very end you will see truly, in fulness of joy.

For this is our Lord's will, that our prayer and our trust be both equally generous. For if we do not trust as much as we pray, we do not pay full honor to our Lord in our prayer, and also we impede and hurt ourselves; and the reason is, as I believe, because we do not truly know that our Lord is the ground from which our prayer springs, and also because we do not know that it is given to us by grace from his love. For if we knew this, it would make us trust to have all we desire from our Lord's gift.

He did not say: You will not be troubled, you will not be belabored, you will not be disquieted; but he said: You will not be overcome. God wants us to pay attention to these words, and always to be strong in faithful trust, in well-being and in woe, for he loves us and delights in us, and so he wishes us to love him and delight in him and trust greatly in him, and all will be well.

*Julian of Norwich, *Showings*, trans. Edmund Colledge, O.S.A., and James Walsh, S.J. (New York: Paulist Press, 1978) 196, 232, 251, 315.

Desire

MANTRA: **My soul is thirsting for you**

SOURCE: Psalm 63

God, you are my God, I am seeking you,
   my soul is thirsting for you,
   my flesh is longing for you,
a land parched, weary and waterless;
I long to gaze on you in the Sanctuary,
   and to see your power and glory.

Your love is better than life itself,
   my lips will recite your praise;
all my life I will bless you,
   in your name lift up my hands;
my soul will feast most richly,
   on my lips a song of joy and, in my mouth, praise.

On my bed I think of you,
I meditate on you all night long,
   for you have always helped me.
I sing for joy in the shadow of your wings;
   my soul clings close to you,
   your right hand supports me.

But may those now hounding me to death
   go down to the earth below,
   consigned to the edge of the sword,
   and left as food for jackals.
then will the king rejoice in God,
and all who swear by him be able to boast
once these lying mouths are silenced.

PARALLEL REFERENCES

There was one of the Pharisees called Nicodemus, a leading Jew, who came to Jesus by night and said, "Rabbi, we know that you are a teacher who comes from God; for no one could perform the signs that you do unless God were with him." (*John 3:1-2*)

His reputation continued to grow, and large crowds would gather to hear him and to have their sickness cured, but he would always go off to some place where he could be alone and pray. (*Luke 5:15-16*)

My soul is thirst-ing for you.

THE THIRST

O Lord my God,
   As parched lips yearn for cool water,
   As baked, barren soil cries out for rain,
   As an empty well pines for the distant spring, so
      MY SOUL IS THIRSTING FOR YOU,
      MY SOUL IS THIRSTING FOR YOU.

O Lord my God,
   As frigid hearts hunger for warm fireside love,
   As frozen January fields long for summer sun,
   As frost-bitten toes dream of pot-belly stoves, so
      MY SOUL IS THIRSTING FOR YOU,
      MY SOUL IS THIRSTING FOR YOU.

O Lord my God,
   As the barren womb pleads for the grace of life,
   As night-eyes await the rays of dawn,
   As untouched hands crave for tender embrace, so
      MY SOUL IS THIRSTING FOR YOU,
      MY SOUL IS THIRSTING FOR YOU.

PRAYER

Lord God, we are a pilgrimage people in search of truth and goodness, peace and joy. We have tasted many waters, pondered many
thoughts, travelled many varied roads. Yet only you, O Lord, can
fill our emptiness. May our thirsting be not in vain; may we not
be deceived by glittering gold. Draw near to us and we shall be
safe—we hunger for your touch.

QUOTATIONS FROM ST. CATHERINE OF SIENA*

If you would make progress, then, you must be thirsty, because
only those who are thirsty are called: "Let anyone who is thirsty
come to me and drink." Those who are not thirsty will never per-
severe in their journey. Either weariness or pleasure will make them
stop. They cannot be bothered with carrying the vessel that would

make it possible for them to draw the water. And though they cannot travel alone, they do not care for the company. So at the first sight of any prick of persecution (which they consider their enemy) they turn back. They are afraid because they are alone. If they were with the company they would not be afraid. And if they had climbed the three stairs they would be secure, because they would not be alone.

Love's second showing is simply in souls themselves, when I show myself to them in loving affection. I do not play favorites but I do respect holy desire, and I show myself in souls in proportion to the perfection with which they seek me. Sometimes I show myself (this is still the second showing) by giving them the spirit of prophecy and letting them see into the future. This can take many forms, depending on what I see to be their need or that of others.

Atonement is made, then, through the desire of the soul who is united to me, infinite Good, in proportion as love is perfect both in the one who prays with desire and in the one who received. And my goodness will measure out to you with the very same measure that you give to me and that the other receives. So feed the flame of your desire and let not a moment pass without crying out for these others in my presence with humble voice and constant prayer. Thus I tell you and the spiritual father I have given you on earth: Behave courageously, and die to all your selfish sensuality.

You see, then, perfect prayer is achieved not with many words but with loving desire, when the soul rises up to me with knowledge of herself, each movement seasoned by the other. In this way she will have vocal and mental prayer at the same time, for the two stand together like the active life and the contemplative life. Still, vocal and mental prayer are understood in many different ways. This is why I told you that holy desire, that is, having a good and holy will, is continual prayer.

Catherine of Siena: The Dialogue, trans. Suzanne Noffke, O.P. (New York: Paulist Press, 1980) 107, 116, 33, 126.

Heart

MANTRA: **Nearest to the Father's heart**

SOURCE: John 1:16-18

Indeed, from his fullness we have, all of us, received—
yes, grace in return for grace,
since, though the Law was given through Moses,
grace and truth have come through Jesus Christ.
No one has ever seen God;
it is the only Son, who is nearest to the Father's heart,
who has made him known.

PARALLEL REFERENCES

"You must not set your hearts on things to eat and things to drink;
nor must you worry. It is the pagans of this world who set their
hearts on all these things. Your Father well knows you need them.
No; set your hearts on his kingdom, and these other things will be
given you as well.
"There is no need to be afraid, little flock, for it has pleased your
Father to give you the kingdom." (*Luke 12:29-32*)

"May they all be one.
Father, may they be one in us,
as you are in me and I am in you,
so that the world may believe it was you who sent me.
I have given them the glory you gave to me,
that they may be one as we are one.
With me in them and you in me,
may they be so completely one
that the world will realize that it was you who sent me
and that I have loved them as much as you loved me." (*John 17:21-23*)

Near-est to the Fa-ther's heart.

HEART TO HEART TALK

NEAREST TO THE FATHER'S HEART,
NEAREST TO THE FATHER'S HEART,
 my only Son, begotten before time,
 my beloved, in whom I am well pleased,
 my chosen one, on whom my favor rests.

NEAREST TO THE FATHER'S HEART,
NEAREST TO THE FATHER'S HEART,
 my faithful steward, gifts carefully tended,
 my obedient servant, the cross fully embraced,
 my humble instrument, rooted in my heart's stream.

NEAREST TO THE FATHER'S HEART,
NEAREST TO THE FATHER'S HEART,
 O Father, your heart is consumed by love.
 O Father, your heart overflows in joy.
 O Father, your heart goes out to every creature.

NEAREST TO THE FATHER'S HEART,
NEAREST TO THE FATHER'S HEART,
 Behold, all nations, such tenderness and peace,
 See, all peoples, the source of all happiness and hope,
 Awake, my soul, and follow Jesus to your true home.

Near - est to the Fa - ther's heart.

PRAYER

Lord Jesus, who lived nearest to the Father's heart, draw us to yourself, thereby drawing us to the nearness of the Father's heart. Let
no space, no time separate us from Love. Yet only you can give us
such entrance, such a privileged dwelling. Lord Jesus, we have lived
far from you—far from your Father's heart—in darkness, in frigid
and harsh lands. Bring us back that we might praise and thank you
every day of our lives. Amen.

QUOTATIONS FROM RALPH WALDO EMERSON*

They found no example and no companion, and their heart fainted.

It is my desire, in the office of a Christian minister, to do nothing which I cannot do with my whole heart.

Speak to his heart, and the man becomes suddenly virtuous.

Without the rich heart, wealth is an ugly beggar.

*The Selected Writings of Ralph Waldo Emerson, ed. Brooks Atkinson (New York: The Modern Library, 1940) 257, 118, 266, 400.

Hope

MANTRA: **For thy sweet love remembered**

SOURCE: William Shakespeare, "When, in disgrace with fortune
and men's eyes"

When, in disgrace with fortune and men's eyes,
I all alone beweep my outcast state,
And trouble deaf heaven with my bootless cries,
And look upon myself, and curse my fate,
Wishing me like to one more rich in hope,
Featured like him, like him with friends possessed,
Desiring this man's art and that man's scope,
With what I most enjoy contented least;
Yet in these thoughts myself almost despising,
Haply I think on thee—and then my state,
Like to the lark at break of day arising
From sullen earth, sings hymns at heaven's gate;
   For thy sweet love remembered such wealth brings
   That then I scorn to change my state with kings.

PARALLEL REFERENCES

Why so downcast, my soul,
why do you sigh within me?
Put your hope in God: I shall praise him yet,
my savior, my God. (*Psalm 42:11*)

"Do not let your hearts be troubled.
Trust in God still, and trust in me.
There are many rooms in my Father's house;
if there were not, I should have told you.
I am going now to prepare a place for you,
and after I have gone and prepared you a place,
I shall return to take you with me;
so that where I am
you may be too." (*John 14:1-3*)

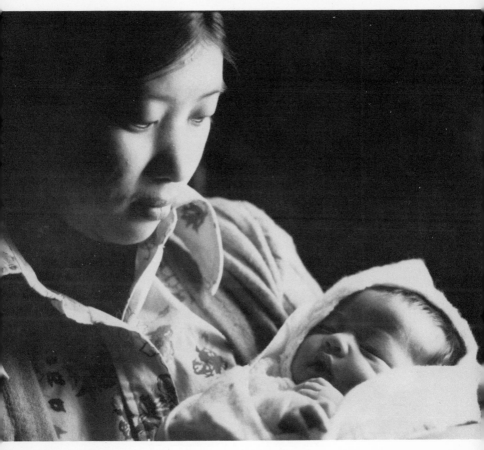

For thy sweet love re-mem-bered.

LIFE-GIVING MEMORIES

the unexpected call, while I sat lazily under the fig tree,
   the surprised cleansing, human feet caressed by divine hands,
      the empty tomb, proud death beaten through obedient love,
         FOR THY SWEET LOVE REMEMBERED!
         FOR THY SWEET LOVE REMEMBERED!

the widow of Naim, eyes moistened with joyful tears,
   the widow of Tagaste, night-long prayers richly fulfilled,
     the widow of Nazareth, suffering love now consoled.
        FOR THY SWEET LOVE REMEMBERED!
        FOR THY SWEET LOVE REMEMBERED!

the gracious well, springs of eternal water and truth,
   the Jericho tree, tax collector exempt from final audit,
     the broken bread, eyes opened to pilgrim's progress,
        FOR THY SWEET LOVE REMEMBERED!
        FOR THY SWEET LOVE REMEMBERED!

thirty pieces of silver, and yet called friend,
   the cock's crow, and yet the forgiving glance,
     the rose crown, and yet no harsh, bitter word.
        FOR THY SWEET LOVE REMEMBERED!
        FOR THY SWEET LOVE REMEMBERED!

For thy sweet love re-mem-bered.

PRAYER

Lord, such wealth we have if we but ponder your movement in our
lives. You continually bless us not only with varied gifts of every
kind but you also give us your very self. We remember your love and
in that remembering are enriched. We are a grateful people.

QUOTATIONS FROM GOETHE*

For friendly crowds that have long been dispersed.
My grief resounds to strangers, unknown throngs
Applaud it, and my anxious heart would burst.
Whoever used to praise my poem's worth,
If they still live, stray scattered through the earth.

Each sees precisely what is in his heart.

Hope never seems to leave those who affirm,
The shallow minds that stick to must and mold—
They dig with greedy hands for gold
And yet are happy if they find a worm.

Since joy on joy crashed on the rocks of time.
Deep in the heart there swells relentless care
And secretly infects us with despair.

Stop playing with your melancholy
That, like a vulture, ravages your breast.

Above all else, it seems to me,
You need some jolly company
To see life can be fun.

*Goethe, *Faust*, trans. Walter Kaufmann (New York: Doubleday & Company, Inc., 1961) 67, 77, 111, 113, 179, 217.

Looking

MANTRA: **Not known, because not looked for**

SOURCE: Thomas Stearns Eliot, "Four Quartets"

We shall not cease from exploration
And the end of all our exploring
Will be to arrive where we started
And know the place for the first time.
Through the unknown, remembered gate
When the last of earth left to discover
Is that which was the beginning;
At the source of the longest river
The voice of the hidden waterfall
And the children in the apple-tree
Not known, because not looked for
But heard, half-heard, in the stillness
Between two waves of the sea.
Quick now, here, now, always—
A condition of complete simplicity
(Costing not less than everything)
And all shall be well and
All manner of thing shall be well
When the tongues of flame are in-folded
Into the crowned knot of fire
And the fire and the rose are one.

PARALLEL REFERENCES

In other words, since they refused to see it was rational to acknowl-
edge God, God has left them to their own irrational ideas and to
their monstrous behavior. And so they are steeped in all sorts of
depravity, rottenness, greed and malice, and addicted to envy,
murder, wrangling, treachery and spite. Libelers, slanderers, enemies
of God, rude, arrogant and boastful, enterprising in sin, rebellious

to parents, without brains, honor, love or pity. They know what God's verdict is: that those who behave like this deserve to die—and yet they do it; and what is worse, encourage others to do the same. (*Romans 1:28-32*)

You were dead, through the crimes and sins in which you used to live when you were following the way of this world, obeying the ruler who governs the air, the spirit who is at work in the rebellious. We all were among them too in the past, living sensual lives, ruled entirely by our own physical desires and our own ideas; so that by nature we were as much under God's anger as the rest of the world. (*Ephesians 2:1-3*)

Not known, be-cause not looked for.

WHAT PRICE IGNORANCE

The distant galaxy hidden beyond fleecy clouds,
Precious gold securely buried in the mountain,
The majestic waterfall hiding its beauty in the rain forest,
    NOT KNOWN, BECAUSE NOT LOOKED FOR,
    NOT KNOWN, BECAUSE NOT LOOKED FOR.

Lofty ideas bound in worn book jackets,
Artistic masterpieces entombed in museum halls,
Enchanting melodies silent in their ancient scores,
    NOT KNOWN, BECAUSE NOT LOOKED FOR,
    NOT KNOWN, BECAUSE NOT LOOKED FOR.

The whisper of God's voice on the desert air,
The touch of the Spirit's breath on warm summer nights,
The gaze of a God-man on parched, dusty road,
    NOT KNOWN, BECAUSE NOT LOOKED FOR,
    NOT KNOWN, BECAUSE NOT LOOKED FOR.

The flight of the morning windhover,
The sunbeam finding an opening in the dawn sky,
The lightning bug darting over the clover fields,
    NOT KNOWN, BECAUSE NOT LOOKED FOR,
    NOT KNOWN, BECAUSE NOT LOOKED FOR.

Not known, be-cause not looked for.

PRAYER

O God, creator of all beauty, I long to discover your presence in
every moment of life and in every work of your hand. Help me to be
attentive and to come to a knowledge of your goodness and mercy.
Heal my blindness, enrich my sight. May your Son Jesus guide me
to you. Amen.

QUOTATIONS FROM TEILHARD DE CHARDIN*

It is essential to see—to see things as they are and to see them really and intensely. We live at the center of the network of cosmic influences as we live at the heart of the human crowd or among the myriads of stars, without, alas, being aware of their immensity. If we wish to live our humanity and our Christianity to the full, we must overcome that insensitivity which tends to conceal things from us in proportion as they are too close to us or too vast.

To repeat: by virtue of the Creation and, still more, of the Incarnation, *nothing* here below is *profane* for those who know how to see.

To the Christian's sensitized vision, it is true, the Creator and, more specifically, the Redeemer (as we shall see) have steeped themselves in all things and penetrated all things to such a degree that, as Blessed Angela of Foligno said, "The world is full of God."

Since my dignity as a man, O God, forbids me to close my eyes to this—like an animal or a child—that I may not succumb to the temptation to curse the universe and him who made it, teach me to adore it by seeing you concealed within it.

*Pierre Teilhard de Chardin, *The Divine Milieu* (New York: Harper and Row, Publishers, 1960) 58-59, 66, 116, 137.

Knowledge

MANTRA: **May I know Thee more clearly**

SOURCE: Prayer of St. Richard

Thanks be to thee, my Lord Jesus Christ,

For all the benefits which thou hast given me,

For all the pains and insults which thou has borne for me,

O most merciful Redeemer, Friend and Brother.

May I know thee more clearly,

Love thee more dearly,

And follow thee more nearly.

PARALLEL REFERENCES

Philip said, "Lord, let us see the Father and then we shall be satisfied." "Have I been with you all this time, Philip," said Jesus to him,
"and you still do not know me?
To have seen me is to have seen the Father,
so how can you say, 'Let us see the Father?'
Do you not believe
that I am in the Father and the Father is in me?
The words I say to you I do not speak as from myself:
it is the Father, living in me, who is doing this work.
You must believe me when I say
that I am in the Father and the Father is in me;
believe it on the evidence of this work, if for no other reason.
I tell you most solemnly,
whoever believes in me
will perform the same works as I do myself,
he will perform even greater works,
because I am going to the Father." (*John 14:8-13*)

Since you have been brought back to true life with Christ, you must look for the things that are in heaven, where Christ is, sitting at God's right hand. Let your thoughts be on heavenly things, not on the things that are on the earth, because you have died, and now the life you have is hidden with Christ in God. But when Christ is revealed—and he is your life—you too will be revealed in all your glory with him. (*Colossians 3:1-4*)

May I know thee more clear - ly.

LEARNING

O Son of God,   dwelling eternally with the Father,
                 embraced by the Father's love,
                 pondering a plan of universal joy,
                 making all things with the Father,
                 saying yes to the dark mystery of the incarnation.
                 MAY I KNOW THEE MORE CLEARLY,
                 MAY I KNOW THEE MORE CLEARLY.

O Jesus,   born in the hill country,
                 nurtured by Mary and Joseph,
                 pondering the silent music of the hills,
                 healing a bent and broken world,
                 bowing in obedience to nail and wood.
                 MAY I KNOW THEE MORE CLEARLY,
                 MAY I KNOW THEE MORE CLEARLY.

O Risen Lord,   traveling down pilgrim roads,
                 invited to meal with newly risen disciples,
                 surprising the fearful in garden and locked room,
                 restoring lost hope and forgotten joy,
                 departing to be present ever again.
                 MAY I KNOW THEE MORE CLEARLY,
                 MAY I KNOW THEE MORE CLEARLY.

May I know thee more clear - ly.

PRAYER

Heavenly Father, reveal your Son to us. Help us to understand his
mind and heart, to live his truth and love. In him we come to know
you and your spirit. Gift us with heart knowledge and then we shall
indeed love ever more dearly and follow ever more nearly.

QUOTATIONS FROM PAUL TILLICH*

There is only one way to know a personality—to become united with that personality through love. Full knowledge presupposes full love. God knows me, because he loves me; and I shall know him face to face through a similar uniting, which is love and knowledge at the same time.

It is not a blind love that is the enduring love, the love that God himself is. It is a seeing love, a knowing love, a love that looks through into the depth of the Heart of God, and into the depth of our hearts. There is no strangeness to love; love knows; it is the only power of complete and lasting knowledge.

For Paul, the difference between knowledge and love, between seeing and acting, between theory and practice, exists only when fragmentary knowledge is our concern.

Paul says that all our present knowledge is like the perception of things in a mirror, that it therefore concerns enigmas and riddles. This is only another way of expressing the fragmentary character of our knowledge.

Those who dream of a better life and try to avoid the Cross as a way, and those who hope for a Christ and attempt to exclude the Crucified, have no knowledge of the mystery of God and of man.

*Paul Tillich, *The Shaking of the Foundations* (New York: Charles Scribner's Sons, 1948) 109, 110, 148.

Time

MANTRA: **A season for everything**

SOURCE: Ecclesiastes 3:1-8

There is a season for everything,
  a time for every occupation under heaven:

 A time for giving birth,
 a time for dying;
 a time for planting,
 a time for uprooting what has been planted.
    A time for killing,
    a time for healing;
    a time for knocking down,
    a time for building.
       A time for tears,
       a time for laughter;
       a time for mourning,
       a time for dancing.
          A time for throwing stones away,
          a time for gathering them up;
          a time for embracing,
          a time to refrain from embracing.
       A time for searching,
       a time for losing;
       a time for keeping,
       a time for throwing away.
    A time for tearing,
    a time for sewing;
    a time for keeping silent,
    a time for speaking.
 A time for loving,
 a time for hating;
 a time for war,
 a time for peace.

PARALLEL REFERENCES

Opposite evil stands good,
opposite death, life;
so too, opposite the devout man stands the sinner.
This is the way to view all the works of the Most High;
they go, in pairs, by opposites. (*Ecclesiasticus 33:14-15*)

"Take the fig tree as a parable: as soon as its twigs grow supple and
its leaves come out, you know that summer is near. So with you
when you see these things happening: know that he is near, at the
very gates." (*Mark 13:28-29*)

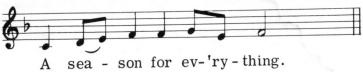

A sea - son for ev-'ry - thing.

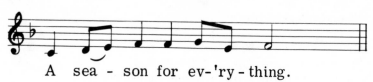

A sea - son for ev-'ry-thing.

A SEASON:

> For April rains and October leaves,
>> for January thaws and July firecrackers,
>>> for June weddings and November funerals,
>>>> THERE IS A SEASON FOR EVERYTHING,
>>>> THERE IS A SEASON FOR EVERYTHING.

> For festive inaugurations and abrupt dismissals,
>> for giddy-up and go . . . to whoa-horse-whoa,
>>> for pistol-crack starts and photo finishes,
>>>> THERE IS A SEASON FOR EVERYTHING,
>>>> THERE IS A SEASON FOR EVERYTHING.

> For arm-wrestling with God and radical obedience,
>> for cross-filled pain and crown-filled victories,
>>> for tongues of fire and bold proclamation,
>>>> THERE IS A SEASON FOR EVERYTHING,
>>>> THERE IS A SEASON FOR EVERYTHING.

> For saying maybe and sometimes if,
>> for dancing polkas and an Irish jig,
>>> for dreaming hopes and pondering loves,
>>>> THERE IS A SEASON FOR EVERYTHING,
>>>> THERE IS A SEASON FOR EVERYTHING.

PRAYER

Gracious and good Father, you who have made the seasons and all that they contain, be present to us at every moment of time and in every place. Regardless of the season, may our faith-filled eyes discern your gentle presence and challenging touch. We thank you for every season of mind and heart, of every time and space.

QUOTATIONS FROM EMILY DICKINSON*

They say that "Time assuages"—
Time never did assuage—
An actual suffering strengthens
As Sinews do, with age—

Time is a Test of Trouble—
But not a Remedy—
If such it prove, it prove too
There was no Malady—

Time feels so vast that were it not
For an Eternity—
I fear me this Circumference
Engross my Finity—

To His exclusion, who prepare
By Processes of Size
For the Stupendous Vision
Of His diameters—

'Twas later when the summer went
Than when the Cricket came—
And yet we knew that gentle Clock
Meant nought but Going Home—
'Twas sooner when the Cricket went
Than when the Winter came
Yet that pathetic Pendulum
Keeps esoteric Time.

Final Harvest. Emily Dickinson's Poems, ed. Thomas H. Johnson (Boston: Little, Brown and Company, 1961) 174, 200, 269.

Happiness

MANTRA: **Always happy in the Lord**

SOURCE: Philippians 4:4-9

I want you to be happy, always happy in the Lord; I repeat, what I want is your happiness. Let your tolerance be evident to everyone: the Lord is very near. There is no need to worry; but if there is anything you need, pray for it, asking God for it with prayer and thanksgiving, and that peace of God, which is so much greater than we can understand, will guard your hearts and your thoughts, in Christ Jesus. Finally, fill your minds with everything that is true, everything that is noble, everything that is good and pure, everything that we love and honor, and everything that can be thought virtuous or worthy of praise. Keep doing all the things that you learned from me and have been taught by me and have heard or seen that I do. Then the God of peace will be with you.

PARALLEL REFERENCES

Happy the man
who never follows the advice of the wicked,
or loiters on the way that sinners take,
or sits about with scoffers,
but finds his pleasure in the Law of Yahweh,
and murmurs his law day and night. (*Psalm 1:1-2*)

Something which has existed since the beginning,
that we have heard,
and we have seen with our own eyes;
that we have touched with our hands:
the Word, who is life—
this is our subject.

That life was made visible:
we saw it and we are giving our testimony,
telling you of the eternal life
which was with the Father and has been made visible to us.
What we have seen and heard
we are telling you so
that you too may be in union with us,
as we are in union
with the Father
and with his Son Jesus Christ.
We are writing this to you to make our own joy complete.

(1 John 1:1-3)

Al - ways hap - py in the Lord.

THE ANCHOR

ALWAYS HAPPY IN THE LORD,
ALWAYS HAPPY IN THE LORD.

ALWAYS, every moment—dawn or dusk,
every season—spring or fall,
every space—peak or valley,
every person—friend or foe,
every service—high or low.

ALWAYS HAPPY IN THE LORD,
ALWAYS HAPPY IN THE LORD.

HAPPY, like trumpets announcing glory!
like eyes aglow with love!
like crystals brilliant in the sun!
like fire embering warmth!
like chestnuts enfolding truth!

ALWAYS HAPPY IN THE LORD,
ALWAYS HAPPY IN THE LORD.

IN THE LORD . . . in the cross of his shared pain,
in the desert of his fierce struggle,
in the temple of his father's glory,
in the house of his blessed people,
in the tomb of his rich poverty.

Al - ways hap - py in the Lord.

PRAYER

The world and our hearts are fickle and fragile, Lord. Happiness
seems distant and fleeting. Grace us to rest always in your loving
presence. Give us the simplicity to see you in all people and events.
Thank you for your many gifts—thank you for being the Giver of
all that is.

QUOTATIONS FROM ST. AUGUSTINE*

Rest in him, and you will in truth have rest. Whither, upon what rough ways, do you wander? Whither do you go? The good you love is from him, but only insofar as it is used for him is it good and sweet. But with justice will it become bitter, if you, as a deserter from him, unjustly love what comes from him. Whither do you walk, farther and farther along these hard and toilsome roads? There is no rest to be found where you seek it; seek what you seek, but it lies not where you seek it. You seek a happy life in the land of death, but it is not there. How can you find a happy life where there is no life?

Lord God of truth, is whoever knows these things by that fact pleasing to you? No, unhappy is the man who knows all this, but does not know you; happy is he who knows you, even if he does not know such things.

In my wretchedness I did not consider from what source it flowed to me that I could discuss so sweetly with my friends these very things, foul as they were. For without friends I could not be happy, even in that frame of mind and with no matter how great a flood of carnal pleasures. In truth, I loved these friends for their own sakes, and I know that they in turn loved me for my own sake.

Far be it, Lord, far be it from the heart of your servant who confesses to you, far be it that, no matter with what joy I may rejoice, I should think myself happy. There is a joy that is not granted to the wicked, but only to those who worship you for your own sake, and for whom you yourself are joy. This is the happy life, to rejoice over you, to you, and because of you: this it is, and there is no other.

* *The Confessions of St. Augustine*, trans. John K. Ryan (New York: Doubleday & Company, 1960) 105, 117, 154-155, 251.

Christk

Finding Christ in every look

Sister Maura, S.S.N.D., "Footnote for a Book of Mystics"

Mystic: a word too loosely flung about,
Whitman and Hopkins, Melville and Donne
and every other man who sometime dared
to look upon the sun.

"The Flaming Heart," "The Tiger," and "The Temple,"
something each poet must have known,
struck some angle of aperture and clung there
staring at the throne.

One more thing—let this relevant detail
be added to the mystics' book:
the sister doling food to dissipated men
and finding Christ in every look.

PARALLEL REFERENCES

The man was anxious to justify himself and said to Jesus, "And who is my neighbor?" Jesus replied, "A man was once on his way down from Jerusalem to Jericho and fell into the hands of brigands; they took all he had, beat him and then made off, leaving him half dead. Now a priest happened to be traveling down the same road, but when he saw the man, he passed by on the other side. In the same way a Levite who came to the place saw him, and passed by on the other side. But a Samaritan traveler who came upon him was moved with compassion when he saw him. He went up and bandaged his wounds, pouring oil and wine on them. He then lifted him on to his own mount, carried him to the inn and looked after him. Next day, he took out two denarii and handed them to the innkeeper.

'Look after him,' he said, 'and on my way back I will make good
any extra expense you have.' Which of these three, do you think,
proved himself a neighbor to the man who fell into the brigands'
hands?" "The one who took pity on him," he replied. Jesus said to
him, "Go and do the same yourself." (*Luke 10:29-37*)

Anyone who says, "I love God,"
and hates his brother,
is a liar,
since a man who does not love the brother that he can see
cannot love God, whom he has never seen. (*1 John 4:20*)

LOST AND FOUND

FINDING CHRIST IN EVERY LOOK
FINDING CHRIST IN EVERY LOOK
finding christ in every look
    the hungry look—blessed are they who hunger for justice,
       the affirming look—you are precious in my sight and I love you,
        the challenging look—come down out of that tree.

FINDING CHRIST IN EVERY LOOK
FINDING CHRIST IN EVERY LOOK
    the despairing look—my God, why have you abandoned me?
      the compassionate look—is there no one here to condemn you?
      the questioning look—who do people say that I am?

FINDING CHRIST IN EVERY LOOK
FINDING CHRIST IN EVERY LOOK
    the radiant look—he was transfigured before their sight,
      the angry look—why have you turned my father's house into
    a den of thieves?
        the honest look—before the cock crows twice you will deny
    me thrice.

Find-ing Christ in ev-'ry look.

PRAYER

O Lord, I have seen your eyes among my friends and acquaintances.
I have looked with your eyes upon others in moments of grace. We
have also looked with other eyes—eyes of cruelty, apathy, and indifference. Help us to see with our hearts so that your presence may
be felt in our days. Fill us with your gentle and warm light. Amen.

QUOTATIONS FROM CARYLL HOUSELANDER*

Why does Christ hide his glory and manifest himself in humility, poverty, and necessity? It is because he must be about his Father's business. His Father's business, the purpose of his life in human creatures, is to love and be loved. Therefore Christ wants to be accessible: He wants to be disarmed of his glory so that the inglorious can come to him without fear, so that he may come to the lowliest and least and be taken to their hearts.

The Child Christ lives on from generation to generation in the poets, very often the frailest of men but men whose frailty is redeemed by a Child's unworldliness, by a child's delight in loveliness, by the spirit of wonder. Christ was a poet, who was King of the invisible kingdom; the priests and rulers could not understand that. The poets understand it, and they, too, are kings of the invisible kingdom, vassal kings of the Lord of Love, and their crowns are crowns of thorns indeed.

It is more in frailty than in strength that Christ reveals himself upon earth; more in littleness than in greatness; more in lowliness than in glory: for he is the Way and such is the Way of Love.

*Caryll Houselander, *The Reed of God* (New York: Sheed & Ward, Inc., 1944) 146, 160, 162.

Meaning

MANTRA: **Would that my tongue could utter**

SOURCE: Alfred, Lord Tennyson, "Break, Break, Break"

Break, break, break,
    On thy cold gray stones, O Sea!
And I would that my tongue could utter
    The thoughts that arise in me.

O well for the fisherman's boy,
    That he shouts with his sister at play!
O well for the sailor lad,
    That he sings in his boat on the bay!

And the stately ships go on
    To their haven under the hill;
But O for the touch of a vanished hand,
    And the sound of a voice that is still!

Break, break, break,
    At the foot of thy crags, O Sea!
But the tender grace of a day that is dead
    Will never come back to me.

PARALLEL REFERENCES

How rich are the depths of God—how deep his wisdom and knowledge—and how impossible to penetrate his motives or understand
his methods! Who could ever know the mind of the Lord? Who
could ever be his counselor? Who could ever give him anything or
lend him anything? All that exists comes from him; all is by him
and for him. To him be glory for ever! Amen. (*Romans 11:33-36*)

This disciple is the one who vouches for these things and has written them down, and we know that his testimony is true.

There were many other things that Jesus did; if all were written down, the world itself, I suppose, would not hold all the books that would have to be written. (*John 21:24-25*)

Would that my tongue could ut - ter.

A WORD

WOULD THAT MY TONGUE COULD UTTER
WOULD THAT MY TONGUE COULD UTTER
   the underground currents of hidden love,
   the unchartered waters of my hesitancy,
   the glacial shifts within my cold heart.

WOULD THAT MY TONGUE COULD UTTER
WOULD THAT MY TONGUE COULD UTTER
   the enticing message of burning autumn leaves,
   the rich pearl of wisdom simply revealed,
   the silent music of the divine milieu.

WOULD THAT MY TONGUE COULD UTTER
WOULD THAT MY TONGUE COULD UTTER
   the quivering pain of eyes filled with hunger,
   the untouchable sore of love unrequited,
   the dreadful hollowness of dignity lost.

WOULD THAT MY TONGUE COULD UTTER
WOULD THAT MY TONGUE COULD UTTER
   the gentle whisper of spring's faithful return,
   the jubilant embrace of friendship restored,
   the exhilarating triumph of a rapids run.

PRAYER

Lord, you have given us a tongue to sing and shout your praise. But you have made reality so much greater than our minds and our lips. Grace us to embrace your mystery and to speak as adequately as we can the mysteries of your love and forgiveness. May Jesus, the risen Lord, utter words that we cannot speak on our own. May glory be yours forever. Amen.

QUOTATIONS FROM HERMANN HESSE*

And who over the ruins of his life pursued its fleeting, fluttering significance, while he suffered its seeming meaninglessness and lived its seeming madness, and who hoped in secret at the last turn of the labyrinth of Chaos for revelation and God's presence?

Ah, look where I might and think what I might, there was no cause for rejoicing and nothing beckoned me. There was nothing to charm me or tempt me. Everything was old, withered, grey, limp and spent, and stank of staleness and decay. Dear God, how was it possible? How had I, with the wings of youth and poetry, come to this: Art and travel and the glow of ideals—and now this! How had this paralysis crept over me so slowly and furtively, this hatred against myself and everybody, this deep-seated anger and obstruction of all feelings, this filthy hell of emptiness and despair.

Learn what is to be taken seriously and laugh at the rest.

It is time to come to your senses. You are to live and to learn to laugh. You are to learn to listen to the cursed radio music of life and to reverence the spirit behind it and to laugh at its distortions. So there you are. More will not be asked of you.

*Hermann Hesse, *Steppenwolf* (New York: Holt, Rinehart and Winston, Inc., 1963) 41, 85, 243, 246-247.

Holiness

MANTRA: **Soul of Christ, sanctify me**

SOURCE: Prayer to Our Redeemer

Soul of Christ, sanctify me.
Body of Christ, save me.
Blood of Christ, inebriate me.
Water from the side of Christ, wash me.
Passion of Christ, strengthen me.
O good Jesus, hear me.
Within thy wounds hide me.
Permit me not to be separated from Thee.
From the wicked foe defend me.
At the hour of my death call me.
And bid me come to Thee
that with thy saints I may praise Thee
for ever and ever. Amen.

PARALLEL REFERENCES

Blessed be God the Father of our Lord Jesus Christ, who in his great mercy has given us a new birth as his children, by raising Jesus Christ from the dead, so that we have a sure hope and the promise of an inheritance that can never be spoiled or soiled and never fade away, because it is being kept for you in the heavens. Through your faith, God's power will guard you until the salvation which has been prepared is revealed at the end of time. This is a cause of great joy for you, even though you may for a short time have to bear being plagued by all sorts of trials; so that, when Jesus Christ is revealed, your faith will have been tested and proved like gold—only it is more precious than gold, which is corruptible even though it bears testing by fire—and then you will praise and glory and honor. You did not see him, yet you love him; and still without seeing him, you are already filled with a joy so glorious that it cannot be described, because you believe; and you are sure of the end to which your faith looks forward, that is, the salvation of your souls.

(1 Peter 1:3-9)

You, my dear friends, must use your most holy faith as your foundation and build on that, praying in the Holy Spirit; keep yourselves within the love of God and wait for the mercy of our Lord Jesus Christ to give you eternal life. *(Jude 20-21)*

Soul   of Christ,   sanc - ti - fy   me.

THE SANCTIFIER

> SOUL OF CHRIST, SANCTIFY ME,
> SOUL OF CHRIST, SANCTIFY ME.

Draw my wandering will into your loving plan,
Heal my vagrant heart by the touch of your hand,
Illumine my darkened mind, life's trials to withstand.

> SOUL OF CHRIST, SANCTIFY ME,
> SOUL OF CHRIST, SANCTIFY ME.

Purify my whys and wherefores by your tender glance,
Cleanse my maybes and ifs with your verbal lance,
Wash my yets and nevers, their power to enhance.

> SOUL OF CHRIST, SANCTIFY ME,
> SOUL OF CHRIST, SANCTIFY ME,

Confirm your peace with a rainbow painting the sky,
Affirm your love with a covenant rung from on high,
Transform your truth as not to exclude the shy.

PRAYER

Father, you desire our sanctification. Make holy our community and institutions by the power of Christ Jesus. May his life, death, and resurrection continue to permeate our history. Possess our fickle souls—draw us into your infinite embrace.

QUOTATIONS FROM MEISTER ECKHART*

Do not think that saintliness comes from occupation; it depends rather on what one is.

God is always ready but we are not ready. God is near to us but we are far from him. God is within; we are without. God is at home; we are abroad.

You must know that God loves the soul so strenuously that to take this privilege of loving from God would be to take his life and being. It would be to kill God, if one may use such an expression. For out of God's love for the soul, the Holy Spirit blooms and the Holy Spirit is that love. Since, then, the soul is so strenuously loved by God, it must be of great importance.

Not to achieve oneness of spirit with God is to fail to be spiritual!

I have sometimes said that if a man goes seeking God and, with God, something else, he will not find God; but if one seeks only God —and really so—he will never find only God but along with God himself he will find all that God is capable of. If you seek your own advantage or blessing through God you are not really seeking God at all.

* *Meister Eckhart*, trans. Raymond Bernard Blakney (New York: Harper & Row, Publishers, 1941) 6, 132, 166, 199, 241.

Witness

MANTRA: **A witness to the peoples**

SOURCE: Isaiah 55:1–5

Oh, come to the water all you who are thirsty;
though you have no money, come!
Buy corn without money, and eat,
and, at no cost, wine and milk.
Why spend money on what is not bread,
your wages on what fails to satisfy?
Listen, listen to me, and you will have good things to eat
and rich food to enjoy.
Pay attention, come to me;
listen, and your soul will live.

With you I will make an everlasting covenant
out of the favors promised to David.
See, I have made of you a witness to the peoples,
a leader and a master of the nations.
See, you will summon a nation you never knew,
those unknown will come hurrying to you,
for the sake of Yahweh your God,
of the Holy One of Israel who will glorify you.

PARALLEL REFERENCES

"Now, Master, you can let your servant go in peace,
just as you promised;
because my eyes have seen the salvation
which you have prepared for all the nations to see,
a light to enlighten the pagans
and the glory of your people Israel." (*Luke 2:29-32*)

Then Yahweh put out his hand and touched my mouth and said to me:
"There! I am putting my words into your mouth.
Look, today I am setting you
over nations and over kingdoms,
to tear up and to knock down,
to destroy and to overthrow,
to build and to plant." (*Jeremiah 1:9-10*)

WITNESSING

I will make you . . .

>Doling food and drink to disheartened people,
>Listening reverently to the story of another's brokenness,
>Soothing the burdened body and the tired mind,
>>A WITNESS TO THE PEOPLE,
>>A WITNESS TO THE PEOPLE.

I will make you . . .

>Nurturing the first grader's sense of wonder and awe,
>Sitting at the bench with the gavel of justice,
>Patrolling the streets with a protective heart,
>>A WITNESS TO THE PEOPLE,
>>A WITNESS TO THE PEOPLE.

I will make you . . .

>Chiseling a manuscript in search of truth and beauty,
>Sweeping the school halls of footprints and smudges,
>Arranging hospital beds for bruised bodies.
>>A WITNESS TO THE PEOPLE,
>>A WITNESS TO THE PEOPLE.

A wit-ness to the peo - ples.

PRAYER

Lord, you are present in all creatures, present to the world in our testimony and witness of your love. Make us fit witnesses of your divine concern. Make us transparent so that through our words and deeds you may be known. May we finish the work that you have given us to do—and thereby give you glory.

QUOTATIONS FROM WALTER BRUEGGEMANN*

No prophet ever sees things under the aspect of eternity. It is always partisan theology, always for the moment, always for the concrete community, satisfied to see only a piece of it all and to speak out of that at the risk of contradicting the rest of it. Empires prefer systematic theologians who see it all, who understand both sides, and who regard polemics as unworthy of God and divisive of the public good.

What takes place when symbols are inadequate and things may not be brought to public expression is that the experience will not be experience.

A prophet has another purpose in bringing hope to public expression, and that is to return the community to its single referent, the sovereign faithfulness of God.

The cross is the ultimate metaphor of prophetic criticism because it means the end of the old consciousness that brings death on everyone. The crucifixion articulates God's odd freedom, his strange justice, and his peculiar power. It is this freedom (read religion of God's freedom), justice (read economics of sharing), and power (read politics of justice) which break the power of the old age and bring it to death. Without the cross, prophetic imagination will likely be as strident and as destructive as that which it criticizes. The cross is the assurance that effective prophetic criticism is done not by an outsider, but always by one who must embrace the grief, enter into the death, and know the pain of the criticized one.

*Walter Brueggemann, *The Prophetic Imagination* (Philadelphia: Fortress Press, 1978) 24-25, 48, 68, 95.

Kingdom

MANTRA: **The smallest of all the seeds**

SOURCE: Matthew 13:31-33

He put another parable before them: "The kingdom of heaven is like a mustard seed which a man took and sowed in his field. It is the smallest of all the seeds, but when it has grown it is the biggest shrub of all and becomes a tree so that the birds of the air come and shelter in its branches."

He told them another parable: "The kingdom of heaven is like the yeast a woman took and mixed in with three measures of flour till it was leavened all through."

PARALLEL REFERENCES

His disciples asked him what this parable might mean, and he said, "The mysteries of the kingdom of God are revealed to you; for the rest there are only parables, so that they may see but not perceive, listen but not understand.

"This, then, is what the parable means: the seed is the word of God. Those on the edge of the path are people who have heard it, and then the devil comes and carries away the word from their hearts in case they should believe and be saved. Those on the rock are people who, when they first hear it, welcome the word with joy. But these have no root; they believe for a while, and in time of trial they give up. As for the part that fell into thorns, this is people who have heard, but as they go on their way they are choked by the worries and riches and pleasures of life and do not reach maturity. As for the part in the rich soil, this is people with a noble and generous heart who have heard the word and take it to themselves and yield a harvest through their perseverance. (*Luke 8:9-15*)

96

He said to them, "Say this when you pray:
'Father, may your name be held holy,
your kingdom come;
give us each day our daily bread,
and forgive us our sins,
for we ourselves forgive each one who is in debt to us.
And do not put us to the test.'" (*Luke 11:1-4*)

The small - est of all   the seeds.

SEEDLINGS

THE SMALLEST OF ALL THE SEEDS,
THE SMALLEST OF ALL THE SEEDS,

A smile—and the graciousness of the kingdom blossoms,
A frown—and the lie blocking the kingdom explodes,
A touch—and the kingdom seems not so far away,
A raindrop—and the barren, arid land is reborn,
A spring sun—and the entombed tree comes back to life.

THE SMALLEST OF ALL THE SEEDS,
THE SMALLEST OF ALL THE SEEDS.

A snowflake—and the kingdom's artist elicits wonder,
A sunbeam—and the light shatters our darkness,
A breeze—and the kingdom touches a new land and a new people,
A sigh—and winter longing catches a second breath,
A shadow—and the Son dispels the fear of death.

THE SMALLEST OF ALL THE SEEDS,
THE SMALLEST OF ALL THE SEEDS.

PRAYER

Lord, you have planted your love in the smallest of all packages.
May we be fertile soil so that our human experiences may bear fruit
to nourish the hungry, comfort the oppressed, bring home the
alienated. Your kingdom come. Your truth, justice, love, and peace
reign!

QUOTATIONS FROM ROMANO GUARDINI*

God's kingdom therefore is no fixed, existing order, but a living,
nearing thing. Long remote, it now advances, little by little, and
has come so close as to demand acceptance. Kingdom of God means
a state in which God is king and consequently rules. What does
this mean?

Let us put it this way: what is it that actually has power over us? What rules me? People, mainly. Those who speak to me, whose words I read; those with whom I associate or would like to associate; the people who give or withhold, who help or hinder me; people I love or influence or to whom I am bound by duty—these rule in me. God counts only when people permit him to, when they and their demands leave me time for him. God rules only in spite of people; when under their influence I am not too strongly tempted to feel that he does not exist at all. He reigns only inasmuch as consciousness of his presence is able to force itself upon me, to coexist with the people in my life. . . . Things also rule in me: things I desire, by the power of that desire; things that bother me, by their bothersomeness; things I encounter wherever I go, by the attraction they have for me or by the attention which they demand. Things in general, by their very existence, fill the spiritual 'space' both within and around me, not God. God is present in me only when the crowding, all-absorbing things of my world leave room for him—either in or through them, or somewhere on the periphery of their existence. No, God certainly does not dominate my life. Any tree in my path seems to have more power than he, if only because it forces me to walk around it! What would life be like if God did rule in me?

God's kingdom is not like the world's, where some command and some obey, where there are quick ones and slow ones, astute and stupid, those who succeed and those who fail. There it is the contrary! Jesus' jubilant words upon his apostles' return from their wonderfully fruitful missions suggests this same idea of complete revaluation: "I praise thee, Father, Lord of heaven and earth, that thou didst hide these things from the wise and the prudent, and didst reveal them to little ones" (*Matt. 11:25-26*).

After the kingdoms of people and things, yes, and in one terrible sense, of Satan, now God's kingdom is to be established. That for which the prophets have waited so long is actually on its way at last—to the chosen people and to all people. The power of God forces itself into the world ready to take over: to forgive, enlighten, lead, sanctify, to transform all things to the new existence of grace.

*Romano Guardini, *The Lord* (Chicago: Henry Regnery Company, 1954) 37-38, 264, 39.

Conversion

MANTRA: **Into stony hearts love flowed**

SOURCE: Ruth Mary Fox, "Carrying Christ"

Into the hillside country Mary went
Carrying Christ, and all along the road
The Christ she carried generously bestowed
His grace on those she met. She had not meant
To tell she carried Christ. She was content
To hide His love for her. But about her glowed
Such joy that into stony hearts love flowed,
And even to the unborn John Christ's grace was sent.

Christ in His Sacrament of love each day
Dwells in my soul a little space and then
I walk life's crowded highway, jostling men
Who seldom think of God. To these I pray
That I may carry Christ, for it may be
Some would not know of Him except through me.

PARALLEL REFERENCES

I am going to take you from among the nations and gather you together from all the foreign countries, and bring you home to your own land. I shall pour clean water over you and you will be cleansed; I shall cleanse you of all your defilement and all your idols. I shall give you a new heart, and put a new spirit in you; I shall remove the heart of stone from your bodies and give you a heart of flesh instead. I shall put my spirit in you, and make you keep my laws and sincerely respect my observances. You will live in the land which I gave your ancestors. You shall be my people and I will be your God. (*Ezekiel 36:24-28*)

100

This is the covenant I will make with the House of Israel when those days arrive—it is Yahweh who speaks. Deep within them I will plant my Law, writing it on their hearts. Then I will be their God and they shall be my people. There will be no further need for neighbor to try to teach neighbor, or brother to say to brother, "Learn to know Yahweh!" No, they will all know me, the least no less than the greatest—it is Yahweh who speaks—since I will forgive their iniquity and never call their sin to mind. (*Jeremiah 31:33-34*)

In - to ston - y hearts love flowed.

HEART OF STONE TO HEART OF FLESH

INTO STONY HEARTS LOVE FLOWED,
INTO STONY HEARTS LOVE FLOWED.
    A word of affirmation—"well done!"
        A song of joy and exaltation.
      A quiet embrace of deepest reverence.
          An assignment of trust and high responsibility.
      An ear that listened behind the word.
      And . . .

INTO STONY HEARTS LOVE FLOWED,
INTO STONY HEARTS LOVE FLOWED.
      An ancient hurt first time shared.
          A dream secretly lodged in the heart of a friend.
    A poem piercing life's crassness.
          A firm, soothing voice calming anxious turbulence.
    A flight of an old dream in November skies.
      And . . .

INTO STONY HEARTS LOVE FLOWED,
INTO STONY HEARTS LOVE FLOWED.

PRAYER

God our Father, Lord of love, the joy of your presence transforms
our hearts. May we recognize your voice at the break of dawn,
may we feel your touch in the cool of the evening, may we do your
will at every moment. The power of the Holy Spirit overwhelms our
fragileness—melt, heal, and restore us. Amen.

To be converted, to be regenerated, to receive grace, to experience religion, to gain an assurance, are so many phrases which denote the process, gradual or sudden, by which a self hitherto divided, and consciously wrong, inferior and unhappy, becomes unified and consciously right, superior and happy, in consequence of its firmer hold upon religious realities.

Conversion is in its essence a normal adolescent phenomenon, incidental to the passage from the child's small universe to the wider intellectual and spiritual life of maturity.

Even late in life some thaw, some release may take place, some bolt be shot back in the barrenest breast, and the man's hard heart may soften and break into religious feeling.

To begin with, there are two things in the mind of the candidate for conversion: first, the present incompleteness or wrongness, the "sin" which he is eager to escape from; and, second, the positive ideal which he longs to compass. Now with most of us the sense of our present wrongness is a far more distinct piece of our consciousness than is the imagination of any positive ideal we can aim at.

So with the conversion experience: that it should for even a short time show a human being what the highwater mark of his spiritual capacity is, this is what constitutes its importance—an importance which backsliding cannot diminish, although persistence might increase it.

*William James, *The Varieties of Religious Experience* (New York: The Modern Library, 1936) 186, 196, 201, 205, 252.

Service

MANTRA: **To serve therewith my maker**

SOURCE: John Milton, "On His Blindness"

When I consider how my light is spent
Ere half my days in this dark world and wide,
And that one talent which is death to hide
Lodged with me useless, though my soul more bent
To serve therewith my Maker, and present
My true account, lest He returning chide;
"Doth God exact day-labor, light denied?"
I fondly ask, But Patience, to prevent
That murmur, soon replies, "God doth not need
Either man's work or his own gifts. Who best
Bear his mild yoke, they serve him best. His state
Is kingly: thousands at his bidding speed,
And post o'er land and ocean without rest;
They also serve who only stand and wait."

PARALLEL REFERENCES

Then I heard the voice of the Lord saying:
"Whom shall I send? Who will be our messenger?"
I answered, "Here I am, send me." He said:
"Go and say to this people,
'Hear and hear again, but do not understand;
see and see again, but do not perceive.'
Make the heart of this people gross,
its ears dull;
shut its eyes,
so that it will not see with its eyes,
hear with its ears,
understand with its heart,
and be converted and healed." (*Isaiah 6:8-10*)

Peter turned and saw the disciple Jesus loved following them—
the one who had leaned on his breast at the supper and said to him,
"Lord, who is it that will betray you?" Seeing him, Peter said to
Jesus, "What about him, Lord?" Jesus answered, "If I want him to
stay behind till I come, what does it matter to you? You are to follow
me." The rumor then went out among the brothers that this disciple
would not die. Yet Jesus had not said to Peter, "He will not die,"
but, "If I want him to stay behind till I come." (*John 21:20-23*)

To serve there-with my Mak - er.

ADSUM (I AM HERE)

TO SERVE THEREWITH MY MAKER,
TO SERVE THEREWITH MY MAKER.

> My ideas—stretched, challenged, anvil forged.
> My affections—purged, refined, x-ray seen.
> My deeds—groping, anxious, lightning tested.
> My memories—stored, catalogued, scrapbook sorted.
> My fantasies—wandering, uncontrolled, kaleidoscope twisted.

TO SERVE THEREWITH MY MAKER,
TO SERVE THEREWITH MY MAKER.

> Our energy—captured power for life and love.
> Our time—fleeting phoenix of beauty and hope.
> Our space—gifted geography of mountains and valleys.
> Our pain—broken nerves welded to the cross.
> Our joy—crowned bliss of divine embrace.

TO SERVE THEREWITH MY MAKER,
TO SERVE THEREWITH MY MAKER.

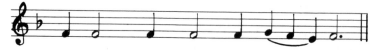

To serve there-with my Mak - er.

PRAYER

Father, our giftedness is meant to serve you and your family. Whatever we have, let it redound to your glory. May we serve you in every way possible, in every moment of time, in every place. Our souls are bent to serve you, our maker, in love and joy. Amen.

QUOTATIONS FROM HANS URS VON BALTHASAR*

This "form" of the Christian—which is, at one and the same time, a pure grace of the Father, his membership of the mystical body of Christ, in fact the man himself taken in his entirety, though in the context of redemption—this form may be called his "mission." To this he should constantly apply all his natural capacities, so that in this surrender to God's service he may find his own supreme fulfillment as a person in a manner surpassing his natural and imperfect potentialities. It is through this that his nature is unfailingly possessed of powers exceeding those proper to it, and so enabled to become truly fruitful.

This response is not "ecstasy," in the sense of violent enthusiasm or a transcending and a rejecting of one's own created reality in order to live outside oneself in God; these two elements may indeed be present, but they are not the core of the experience. Rather, it is primarily adoration of the infinite holiness of God present in the soul, and this adoration implicitly contains assent to being wholly possessed by God for his own purposes; it is "ecstasy," indeed, but the ecstasy of service, not of enthusiasm.

A third group of counsels emphasizes the ordinary virtues that proceed from love. The supreme moments of blissful intercourse are not many in the life of lovers; they spend the greater part of their lives separate, in their respective duties and work. It is here that love must prove its strength; it becomes loyalty, patience and humble service.

*Hans Urs von Balthasar, *Prayer*, trans. A. V. Littledale (New York: Sheed & Ward, 1961) 49, 64, 110.

Oneness

MANTRA: **Make us one with you always**

SOURCE: Oration for 14th Sunday in Ordinary Time

Father,
in the rising of your Son
death gives birth to new life.
The sufferings he endured restored hope to a fallen world.
Let sin never ensnare us
with empty promises of passing joy.
Make us one with you always,
so that our joy may be holy,
and our love may give life.
We ask this through Christ our Lord. Amen.

PARALLEL REFERENCES

The whole group of believers was united, heart and soul; no one claimed for his own use anything that he had, as everything they owned was held in common. (*Acts 4:32*)

If our life in Christ means anything to you, if love can persuade at all, or the Spirit that we have in common, or any tenderness and sympathy, then be united in your convictions and united in your love, with a common purpose and a common mind. That is the one thing which would make me completely happy. There must be no competition among you, no conceit; but everybody is to be self-effacing. Always consider the other person to be better than yourself, so that nobody thinks of his own interests first but everybody thinks of other people's interests instead. In your minds you be the same as Christ Jesus. (*Philippians 2:1-5*)

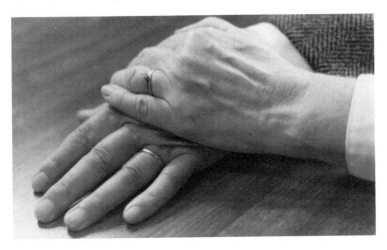

Make us one with you al - ways.

UNITY

MAKE US ONE WITH YOU ALWAYS,
MAKE US ONE WITH YOU ALWAYS.

Divine Shepherd—bring your scattered sheep home,
Divine Mender—call our sins never to mind,
Divine Surgeon—reset our broken heart in love,
Divine Counselor—share your tender feelings of compassion,
Divine Father—tell us again the story of your son.

MAKE US ONE WITH YOU ALWAYS,
MAKE US ONE WITH YOU ALWAYS.

Divine Mediator—arbitrate our hatred and our wars,
Divine King—govern our complex impulses and motives,
Divine Prophet—proclaim your justice to all the nations,
Divine Savior—heal our fragile, weary world,
Divine Spirit—grant us trust and joy.

MAKE US ONE WITH YOU ALWAYS,
MAKE US ONE WITH YOU ALWAYS.

PRAYER

God, our loving Father, you are the wellspring of life. Our hearts long to be one with you; our spirits hunger for your touch. May our divisions cease, our resentment and bitterness be forgiven, our pettiness be cauterized. Lord Jesus, may we be one with you as you are one with the Father.

QUOTATIONS FROM NIKOS KAZANTZAKIS*

What miracle life is and how alike are all souls when they send their roots down deep and meet and are one!

We stayed silent by the brazier until far into the night. I felt once more how simple and frugal a thing is happiness: a glass of wine, a roast chestnut, a wretched little brazier, the sound of the sea. Nothing else. And all that is required to feel that here and now happiness is a simple, frugal heart.

"Because God, you know, is a great lord, and that's what being a lord means: to forgive!"

"I think, Zorba—but I may be wrong—that there are three kinds of men: those who make it their aim, as they say, to live their lives, eat, drink, make love, grow rich, and famous; then come those who make it their aim not to live their own lives but to concern themselves with the lives of all men—they feel that all men are one and they try to enlighten them, to love them as much as they can and do good to them; finally there are those who aim at living the life of the entire universe—everything, men, animals, trees, stars, we are all one, we are all one substance involved in the same terrible struggle. What struggle? . . . Turning matter into spirit."

"Alexis," he said, "I'm going to tell you a secret. You're too small to understand now, but you'll understand when you are bigger. Listen, little one: neither the seven stories of heaven nor the seven stories of earth are enough to contain God, but a man's heart can contain him. So be very careful, Alexis—and may my blessing go with you—never to wound a man's heart!"

*Nikos Kazantzakis, *Zorba the Greek* (New York: Simon and Schuster, Ballentine Books, Inc., 1952) 78, 93, 121, 309-310.

More books by Bishop Morneau—

MANTRAS FOR THE MORNING
An Introduction to Holistic Prayer

Bishop Morneau's first collection of mantras established the content and form followed in this book, *Mantras for the Evening*. The themes of the morning mantras include newness, listening, pleasing God, the smile, spring, fellowship, presence, beloved, intimacy, simplicity, confession, praise, silence, renewal, and indwelling. Each theme is enhanced with biblical and literary passages, music, and photos to bring freshness and wholeness to meditative prayer. *120 pages, softbound, $4.25. A 1981 publication.*

OUR FATHER REVISITED

The author begins his book of prayer where Jesus began when he said, "When you pray say, 'Our Father, . . .'" Dividing this prime prayer into eight sections, Bishop Morneau offers four reflections on each part, thereby providing rich material for four hours of meditation during eight days. Practical notes on five principles of prayer introduce this ideal companion for a private, directed, or traditional retreat. *78 pages, softbound, $2.95. A 1978 publication.*

TRINITY SUNDAY REVISITED
Patterns for Prayer

Not the liturgical feast, but the poem "Trinity Sunday" by George Herbert, a seventeenth-century poet, is the source of these 32 themes for prayer. The themes are gathered into an eight day framework for easy use during a retreat or a monthly day of reflection. The author prefaces these prayer-days with ten principles of prayer. *96 pages, softbound, $2.95. A 1980 publication.*

DISCOVERING GOD'S PRESENCE

Fifteen prayerful articles lead the reader to an ever-new, ever-deeper discovery of God's presence in poetry, prayer, struggle, success, living, playing, dying—all in the spirit of surprise at our many-splendored God. Here is proof—if we need it—that the old catechism was right when it said, "God is everywhere." *187 pages, softbound, $5.95. A 1980 publication.*

THE LITURGICAL PRESS
Collegeville, Minnesota 56321

More books on prayer—

RUNWAYS TO GOD: The Psalms as Prayer *by Fr. Paschal Botz, O.S.B.* This valuable help in praying the psalms gives the text of and concise commentary on the 150 psalms, the Church's oldest and most solid prayers. *354 pages, softbound, $4.75.*

BREAD IN THE WILDERNESS *by Thomas Merton.* The well known Trappist explores the prayer-power of the psalms with such themes as "Psalms and Contemplation," "From Praise to Ecstasy," and "The Silence of the Psalms." *126 pages, softbound, $3.00.*

BIBLICAL PRAYER *by Fr. Ernest Lussier, S.S.S.* This clear, concise, and comprehensive consideration of prayer in the Old and New Testaments emphasizes the forms, the action, and the efficacy of prayer. *138 pages, softbound, $3.50.*

OUR FAMILY PRAYS *by Fr. Simeon Thole, O.S.B.* This handy prayerbook series contains a wide variety of ten-minute family prayer sessions of readings and meditations on the Gospels. Available in the following editions according to the liturgical seasons: Ordinary Time, Advent and Christmas, Lent and Easter. *64 pages, softbound, $.50.*

CHRIST IN US: Reflections on Redemption *by Fr. Alban Boultwood, O.S.B.* The author's reflections on redemption, the Eucharist, the theological virtues, holiness, loneliness, work, prayer, and other topics provide fresh, abundant material for meditation and inspiration. The 45 short selections are solidly based on Scripture and set in the framework of the liturgical year. *144 pages, softbound, $5.50.*

SHARING GOD'S LOVE *by Fr. John Marshall, O.F.M.* Twenty-five pointed and pithy chapters focus attention on such topics as prayer, gratitude, faith, honesty, prophecy, priesthood, the Eucharist, justice, suffering, and wisdom. These are the ways and means God shares his love with us. *108 pages, softbound, $5.95.*

LITURGY MADE SIMPLE *by Mark Searle.* Prayer should be at its best when the Church, the Body of Christ, prays publicly. This clearly written explanation of the Mass is certain to deepen the reader's understanding of and appreciation for the Eucharistic celebration. *96 pages, softbound, $2.95.*

THE LITURGICAL PRESS
Collegeville, Minnesota 56321